The Coachman

Noël Le Breton de Hauteroche

Translated
with an introduction by
Edwin L. Isley

Seventeenth-century Press

For Donald W. Gilman

Preface to *The Coachman* (1684) by Noël Le Breton, sieur de Hauteroche

Noël Le Breton, known as Hauteroche, had an illustrious career in the theatre as an actor, administrator, and a playwright. It was he who provided, from the company of four actor-playwrights—including Raymond Poisson, Guillaume Marcoureau de Brécourt, and Charles Chevillet Champmeslé—the greatest number of new plays for the theatre of the Hôtel de Bourgogne, the theatre that became the chief rival of that of Molière and his company. Very few playwrights have had such contemporary admiration and such a loyal following as Hauteroche.

The considerable success in the theatre of Hauteroche's *L'Esprit folet ou La Dame invisible* in February 1684 was followed up with another in the summer season. In early June (7 or 9?) *The Coachman* (*Le Cocher*), Hauteroche's eleventh play, was given its first performance and successful run of twelve consecutive performances, then played repeatedly in counterpoint with the summer's season's other outstanding dramatic success, Brécourt's *Timon ou les flatteurs trompés* (1684).[1] It was performed before the court at Fontainebleau in September and reprised in the city in December. For the leading *rôle* of Morille, the coachman of the title, Poisson was again enlisted, further assurance of the popular success of the play evidently sought by the playwright in his choice of form and source.[2]

Hauteroche drew again on a Spanish source, Antonio Hurtado de Mendoza's *Los Riesgos que tiene un coche* (1653) and proceeded to adapt it to contemporary taste in the same manner he had used in his rewriting of Calderón for his own *L'Esprit folet ou La Dame invisible*.[3] He frankly boasts, in his *Avis* to the first printing of *The Coachman* that his version is theatrically superior to his predecessor's, and critical opinion has ratified his claim. The Parfaict brothers struck the first laudatory note, echoed by virtually all subsequent commentators. Clean lines of narrative development in plotting, as is in fact necessary for the successful rhythm and pace of the one-act play, comes first in praise, accompanied by an acknowledgement of novelty in conception of the subject—the coachman's disguise—as well as the characterization of Hilaire, the potentially stock tyrannical "father figure", that is the principal partner for Morille's performance. While Hauteroche may have been inspired, consciously or not, by an episode from Molière's *Monsieur de Pourceaugnac* (1669) (thus leaving a little of Limoges in the new play), in the kind of carnivalesque scene that obviously attracted his attention and admiration, that "source" in no way lessens the personal way in which Hauteroche dramatizes that one strand of Molière's tangled web set for his Limousin up from the country. [4]

The Coachman is most famous for the scene in which Morille, in disguise as a coachman, is confronted by an unknown woman disguised as his wife. The resources of Poisson's performance style are fully exploited, from the first eye rolls of alarmed surprise to leers and the gestures of lecherously roving hands, as the all-too-willing Hilaire directs the scene he himself sets in the privacy of a *cabinet* in his comfortably appointed house and Morille's reactions from physical alarm to concupiscent promise.

This comic high point is the intersection of two schemes involving Hilaire and his household. The first ruse unfolds in the introduction and is the young lover Lisidor's scheme. Le Mans replaces Limoges, but the effect is the same: a provincial in the city, moving from the street and its life into a place he would make his own, encumbered by his country attachments. These do not include here, for

Lisidor and Morille, any more than they had for Molière's Pontignan and Scapin (*Les Fourberies de Scapin* (1671)), the linguistic impediment of a provincial accent, which is left once and for all to the episodic, functional *rôles* of lower status servants, often designated by names suggesting their particular province and embodying a single popularly recognizable trait of that province (like Breton drunkenness). A *fiancée*, with a letter to prove her claim, to whom he has declared himself passionately attached, is Lisidor's principal encumbrance. It is she who sets herself on Morille, disguising as his wife. After having decided that no news is bad news and that Lisidor has been away an alarmingly long time, she has, unknown to him, come to Paris in pursuit. Once there she has set the younger brother of her maid, one Adrian, to spy on Lisidor. He confirms her worst suspicions that Lisidor has in fact strayed, in the amorous pursuit of the fair Dorothée, Hilaire's niece, destined, she (by her uncle), for the less than fair Eutrope, a clumsy but smitten suitor, a man of a certain age and of the law, with whom Hilaire might face a lawsuit, were it not for the mollifying promise of the gift of his niece's hand in marriage.

Before the moment that Julie hatches her plot to gain entry into Hilaire's household, and sets in motion the scheme for revenge if not the renewal of relations with Lisidor, the second of the two schemes that intersect in Hilaire's *cabinet*, Julie's action had already contributed to the disorder besetting Hilaire's established life and plans that will play itself on this day of comedy. With her blessing, Adrian has sent an anonymous letter to Hilaire, exposing Dorothée's trysts with an unknown gentleman while driving in the park. Moreover, Eutrope has also come by this incriminating evidence, through Hilaire's own divulging of it. This sticky situation, for all concerned, has not been aided by Hilaire's mismanaged confrontation of Dorothée, who will admit to nothing and slips out of his control by negative assent on the matter of his niece doing her duty (of marrying Euthrope). Hilaire does the "heavy father" badly, allowing himself to be manipulated into a lie (that he himself has seen the trysts, when in fact he has only the second-hand, dubious authority of an anonymous letter) and finally violence, in the act claustrating Dorothée until her marriage. Her coolness to this threat, further frustration for Hilaire, signifies that she considers it an empty one not to be taken seriously. Such is the preliminary state of affairs in the Hilaire domain at the moment Julie imagines her scheme, and we have reached a second stage in the farce: the physical penetration of Lisidor into Hilaire's house.

It is only then that the spectator is fully aware that Morille, seen to be in Lisidor's service from the opening scene, is in disguise as a coachman. In his first "real" scene, with Hilaire, the coachman had performed a comedy of unfittingness and of discrepancy, which is just one aspect of the frustrating disorder sprung upon Hilaire, who comes to the same communicational impasse with his servant that he will undergo with his niece. Trying to elicit information on the trysts and the identity of the unknown gentleman from him, Hilaire meets a stone wall in a display of "professional pride" and knowing one's place; the argument is frustratingly unbeatable: "Monsieur, j'aime me taire, que de mal parler". Morille has learned the wisdom that Molière's Sosie is given by experience and reiterates it in his show of worthiness: "Monsieur, il ne faut jamais qu'un serviteur mette le nez dans les affaires de ceux dont il mange le pain, à moins qu'ils ne l'ordonnent." To this repeated plain speech (but a verbal "mask" nonetheless), Hilaire can only respond with a mixed salad of expletives that at least signal his growing anger: "Le diable t'emporte," "Que le Ciel te confonde," "Que la foudre t'écrase," "Maraut," and "Bourreau".

The revelation that Morille is not in fact a coachman at all is a virtual *coup de théâtre* realized more fully by the cutting of the *supposé* from the primitive title of the play—*Le Cocher supposé* and enhanced by the verbal comedy of Morille's "confession" to Dorothée. He has had no previous experience with horses, "moi qui n'avois en ma vie mène de carosse. Je vous tiens fort heureuse, que mon ignorance ne vous ait point fait casser le cou, ou quelque membre." Then he waxes eloquent, stripping himself down, once the process has begun, to a comic speech that parodies with its chosen ornaments, the plain speech offered in turn to Lisidor, Hilaire, and here first to Dorothée: "Quant à moi, je suis d'avis de demander mon congé, car le métier de Cocher, que je fais malgré moi pour servir vos amours, m'attirera sans doute quelque maligne influence. Tout franc, je crains la destinée de Monsieur Phaëton; c'est-à-dire que la foudre de votre Oncle a déjà commencé par un soufflet, à faire le Jupiter sur mon Visage". His direct question to Dorothée—"Mais aujourd'huy puis-je joüer un autre rôle, sans que votre Oncle s'en aperçoive?"—is answered by Julie's scheme and its new *rôle* of husband, and he, like Hilaire, will be cast into the new scenario, "sans qu'il s'en aperçoive."

The inspired nature of Julie's cleverness, and with it the comic playwright's, is underscored by a scene of similar circumstances in Julie's retinue to that played by Morille and Dorothée. She and her maid, Rosette, and Rosette's brother Adrian have also come to an impasse, now that the second sequence of scenes has led to the second, critical stage of Lisidor's progress. They have seen, in the traditional square of streets before two houses that constitutes Hauteroche's stage set, the entry themselves, through Morille's quarters. Sympathetic and indignant for her mistress, Rosette would avenge herself for a betrayal like Lisidor's by violence: "Tout franc, si j'aimois comme vous aimez, j'aurois déjà mis le feu à la maison." Getting even, not mad, is more Julie's way: her retort—"La violence est ici bien moins necessaire que l'adresse". Rosette continues to indulge her fantasies of getting in her licks: "Morguenne, il s'en souviendroit. Mais que prétendez-vous faire? Quant à moi, j'enrage de battre. Ah! que je prendrois un grand plaisir à bourrer un infidèle, & à lui faire retourner dans le ventre sa perfidie & son inconstance." During this tirade Julie drifts off in a reverie that is the state of grace visited by comic inspiration and the *trouvaille* of the perfect scheme—the light bulb proverbially coming on in the bubble over the head of characters in illustrated cartoons—assured by Hauteroche's stage direction: "après avoir un peu rêvé." "Cesse tes emportements, baisse ta coësse," she commands her troop as she swings actions into strategy and knocks decisively at Hilaire's door.

The *quid pro quo* of the masquerade is fleshed out with the kind of bawdiness that traditionally spices farce. It is set up through Hilaire, who has only to lay eyes on Julie, "wife of Morille," to be won over to her cause of abandoned wife and mother. To her clarification, "Il est mon mari." He answers: "Il n'est pas digne de ce nom-là, & vous méritez une autre fortune," and in response to Julie's modest acknowledgement of the compliment, he is moved to pledge his support: "Je veux prendre votre parti contre lui, & par-là vous donner des marques sensibles de l'estime que j'ai pour vous". Her profession of gratitude pushes him even farther, into at least the third instance of his extravagant and hair-triggered violence and passion. "Votre abord m'a touché d'une telle manière, que je l'étranglerois s'il refusoit à faire son devoir auprès de vous." After a rapid glance at Rosette, Julie's new "cousin," elicits only an *assez jolie* by comparison, Hilaire ushers Madame into the *cabinet* as though stepping in for the unworthy husband: "Elle est assez jolie, mais tout franc,

ix

vous l'êtes encore plus qu'elle. Je vais faire ouvrir mon appartement, pour vous y faire entrer & là nous expliquerons avec lui de bonne manière".

Rosette is quick to spy and to point out the extent to which Julie's seduction scene has succeeded, "Ma foi, Madame, je crois que ce Monsieur Hilaire se sent remuer... dans lui... quelque chose pour vous". The time—thirty years—has long passed when the coyness of this kind of omissions and their sexual innuendo scandalized *bien pensant* spectators of Molière's *L'École des femmes* (1662). The character of the figure of Adrian, characterized by his sister as in anybody's pay to supplement his winnings from gambling—*guère honnêté*—is alone evidence enough that we have entered the world of the Paris street fairs and con games in which Florent Carton Dancourt's plays are set or their only lightly veiled transformation in the Naples of Molière's *Les Fourberies de Scapin* that already resituates virtually within the farce a new audience for it. What is coyly understated in Rosette's identification is significantly shrugged off in response by Julie's "*Qu'importe.*" That Julie plays at seduction for her own ends means less to the spectator, or is totally obscured for him, by the progress of her charms, *sensiblement* felt by two men—as Morille in his turn falls. The comic grace of performance effects an enactment of poetic justice to the point that Julie wins over spectators to her cause as rapidly as she does the conversions on stage.

Morille's lechery, which succeeds his first puzzled reactions, insulted as he is and even laid hands on by Hilaire, is a fantasy invited by the ambiguous direction of the overzealous and clumsy Hilaire in his *rôle* of reconciler and marriage counsellor. "Te voilà tout interdit, coquin! Allons qu'on l'embrasse tout-à-l'heure devant moi; qu'on lui témoigne son repentir, & qu'on la prie de vouloir te pardonner. (À Julie) Le voulez-vous pas bien," Hilaire initially invites them. To which Julie replies with equal ambiguity: "Tout ce qu'il vous plaira, Monsieur". Then, as they warm to their task, Hilaire bids the couple to join hands: "Mais pour l'amour de moi, touchez-vous dans la main," and Julie adds: "J'obéis à vos ordres avec bien du plaisir". As for Morille, he admits that he still is in the dark: "Parbleu, je n'y vois goutte." It takes Hilaire's added directions to wake him up: "Votre réunion ne sera pas bien faite que vous n'ayez couché ensemble." "Je voudrois voir cela," Morille rapidly replies, a response that is a line direction for Poisson's signature wide-eyed mugging. Julie plays for time—"rien ne presse, Monsieur," giving no hint in voice and demeanor that her scheme may in fact be undergoing some serious complications. The time serves Hilaire for some further fantasizing: "J'en demeure d'accord; mais dans ces sortes de réconciliation, le particulier de l'homme & de la femme est un grand secours pour terminer bien des contestations. Vous pouvez, en attendant mieux, disposer de ce cabinet, vous y déshabillez, & vous mettre au lit." Morille instantly starts to undo his buttons, while Hilaire approves his dispatch. Regretfully the willing voyeur must avert his eyes, in effect leave, as he makes ready to do and to take Rosette with him. "Sans façon je veux vous voir ensemble dans le lit," he begins, then adds: "& pour cela il faut vous laisser seule avec votre époux; l'occasion achèvera de cimenter ce que j'ai mis en beau chemin". Julie manages to keep Rosette at her side while dismissing Hilaire, and it is, in fact, she who closes the door. With its slam she issues a *faquin* at Morille that is the beginning of a new lesson on reality, the first of the play's last sequence of scenes.

Put on trial by the two women for his *fourberies*, read into evidence by Julie, Morille cannot retreat to his former *rôle* of coachman. His lies are instantly identified and punished by a slap from Rosette, to punctuate her mistress' *l'effronté menteur.* Threatened with repeated punishment for further lies, and the demand to reveal Lisidor's whereabouts, Morille struggles to escape. Julie, who preferred and supposedly still does brain to brawn, loses her composure—"Ah, maraut, il faut que je t'étrangle" and joins in the assault of blows on one side that Rosette has begun on the other. The noise of this all-enveloping farce draws Hilaire back, and Morille is given a second lesson in reality: he is no more believed by Hilaire than by the women; he cannot win his case. It takes only the false accusation of the "battered wife," in explanation of the noise to Hilaire, to indict Morille, who in the event cannot lie skillfully enough to counteract the potentially as threatening exposure of the man hiding introduced by him into Hilaire's domicile. Hilaire simpers in gratitude to Julie, "la caressant," according to Hauteroche's stage direction: "Que ne vous dois-je point!" Julie has the last word: "Si vous voulez que je vous dise davantage, faites venir cet homme en ce lieu, & que devant eux vous soyez instruit de toute chose." The only thing that stands in the way of a rapid *dénouement* at this point is a bit of farce.

In preparation for the actual *dénouement* of the *scène dernière*, Morille profits from the little bit of time given him to humble himself and to throw himself upon the mercy of the women, first of Rosette, to whom his appeal takes the form of a renewed courtship, seemingly begun long ago in Le Mans. She shows that she does not have a heart of stone and in her turn so does Julie, who accedes to Rosette's plea for Morille's forgiveness. Dorothée is heard approaching and, once apprised of the situation, issues an equally human response: "O Ciel, que je suis malheureuse!" The promise of happy resolution and the threat of its undoing combine to underscore the tension that remains up to the *dénouement*. It resides in the anticipation of Hilaire's response to the truth and his reactionary course of action in settling the disorder created by both schemes that have caused it—for the time it has taken to play them out on stage, since Hauteroche has given the farce the optimum time structure of full congruence of fictional chronology and playing time.

Exposure and forgiveness, or at least probation, unfold so quickly that the formal *dénouement* passes by the spectator in a flash of actions. Hilaire's judgments, once the characters' true identities have been revealed to him, are unmercifully terse and surprisingly effective, untroubled as might have been expected by wounded pride and vanity. Exposed as an intruder, and a *fourbe* in fact, Lisidor fails to stand up for himself (Morille has in fact cleared the way for this by refusing one last time to deliver himself of a judgment). Lisidor will say only "Que cela peut être vrai, & peut être faux." Hilaire, equally terse and understated, replies only that "La réponse est un peu normande," before turning the case over to Dorothée to judge. His "Et vous votre Nièce, qu'en dîtes-vous?" is from every point of view unexpected. Perhaps his niece is not unexpected to him, with obvious disdain, she denounces Lisidor with her judgment—"Que c'est un fourbe, un scélérat, que je déteste"—and exits with the line. Lisidor is expelled (and Morille with him) by Hilaire with threats of the law if he does not go forthwith. Before going, he kneels to ask Julie's forgiveness, which comes, as prepared by her earlier pardoning of Morille, without resistance. Her heart is intact. Hilaire is untouched by the spectacle, and by Julie's apology for the inconvenience they have all cause him, and also orders Julie and Rosette from his house. At the same time he deals with his niece's future, and with Morille. "Allez au diable & sortez promptement de mon logis. Pour ma Nièce, elle époüsera dès demain Eutrope, ou un Couvent. (À Morille lui donnant un soufflet en sortant) & pour toi voilà ton salaire." The last words are Morille's, first a "Me voilà payé de mes gages," which inevitably resonates with the famously final words of Sganarelle in Molière's *Dom Juan ou le festin de pierre* (1665)—"Et mes gages?" But significantly there is no question in Morille's remark concerning this fact in the settling up of his idea of the natural order of things. Finally, as the newly happy lovers prepare to exit, Rosette awaits Morille's arm, he echoes with renewed knowledge his own judgment, however askew its expression as voiced: "Je vous suis; car il ne fait pas bon ici pour moi".

Physically absent from the *dénouement* is Eutrope, who is waiting in the wings (Dorothée's *apartment*) as Dorothée's future. Like Lisidor, he has entered into the house; unlike the young adventurer, he has been invited. Eutrope, who was last seen on stage wandering through and voicing the play's only monologue, is after all not so bad a fellow, lost as he was last seen in his calf-like love, not a fate worse than death or its equivalent in a life sentence to a convent. Accustomed as spectators have become to the parade of clever young women characters that Hauteroche sends across his stage in 1684, some of the spectators may have left *The Coachman* with a smile accompanying the thought that well, after all she is not married yet... . Such trailing, post-performance projections represent one proof, by *infection*, as it were, of the triumphant imposition of a personal style, *la comédie hauterochienne*.

Edwin L. Isley

THE COACHMAN,[1]

COMEDY.

CHARACTERS.

Mr. HILAIRE, *Dorothée's uncle.*

Mr. EUTROPE, *Dorothée's lover.*

LISIDOR, *Dorothée's other lover.*

DOROTHÉE, *Lisidor's lover, and promised to Mr. Eutrope.*

JULIE, *Lisidor's lover.*

ROSETTE, *Julie's servant.*

ROLINE, *Dorothée's servant.*

MORILLE, *Lisidor's valet, and Mr. Hilaire's coachman.*

ADRIAN, *Rosette's brother.*

The scene is in Paris, in Mr. Hilaire's house.

THE COACHMAN,

COMEDY.

FIRST SCENE.

LISIDOR, MORILLE.

MORILLE.

Oh, sir, I was just looking for you.

LISIDOR.

And, Morille, I was trying to catch up with you. Why were you looking for me?

MORILLE.

For two reasons: one, to let you know that yesterday I ran into one of my friends from Le Mans,[2] who told me that dear Rosette sends her love, and who informed me that Ms. Julie is distressed at your delay in Paris; she knows that your business was completed some time ago and that you should have already returned.

LISIDOR.

I know that. Don't you have anything else to tell me?

MORILLE.

Yes, I do, but, sir, Julie is a person who...

2

LISIDOR.

Enough about Julie, tell me about Dorothée.

MORILLE.

Read this note, and let me go! Someone may come from the house… I'm your humble servant.

LISIDOR.

You're right. Go! (*He reads.*)

I'll go for a walk now to the Invalides;[3] and hope to find you there. I'll go early so that I may enjoy being with you even longer. Goodbye until then; always love me as much as I love you, DOROTHÉE.

I see her uncle coming. Let's get away from here!

SCENE II.

HILAIRE, EUTROPE.

EUTROPE.

Rest assured, Mr. Hilaire, it's true.

HILAIRE.

I confess, Lord Eutrope, that I can hardly believe what you just told me.

EUTROPE.

Yet nothing is more certain.

HILAIRE.

But, Lord Eutrope, couldn't it just be jealousy that has fed your imagination? Often lovers who are insecure take the shadow for substance and the lie for the truth.

EUTROPE.

Again, Mr. Hilaire, it's the truth.

HILAIRE.

But from whom are you getting the information?

EUTROPE.

A sealed note was sent to my house, during my absence, without any indication of its origins. I can't even recognize the handwriting.

HILAIRE.

This may be true or a story made up just for the fun of it.

EUTROPE.

No, nothing is more certain! I am completely convinced!

HILAIRE.

Could we have a look at the note?

EUTROPE.

Certainly, here it is.

HILAIRE *reads.*

To Mr. Eutrope.

I'm concerned about something which compels me to warn you that Ms. Dorothée, Mr. Hilaire's niece, with whom you are passionately in love, loves a horseman who is unknown to you, and they meet every day at the promenade. If you doubt what I'm writing, you can, with a little care, easily verify this for yourself.

EUTROPE.

I did exactly that, and I saw her yesterday in the Bois de Vincennes,[4] speaking with an unknown gentleman.

HILAIRE.

Outside of the carriage?

EUTROPE.

Yes, outside of the carriage and walking with him rather casually.

HILAIRE.

You have surprised me. I want to clear up this business with you immediately. I must confront her about this.

EUTROPE.

No, that's not what I want; I don't want her to become angry with me, and I believe that she would find it presumptuous if I were to admonish her for her actions when I am not yet her husband; I don't even want her to know that this information came from me; I know her mind, and...

HILAIRE.

That's enough, I understand, Lord Eutrope; do you love my niece?

EUTROPE.

Of course I do, to think otherwise is to insult me.

HILAIRE.

Lord Eutrope, I promised you my niece, and I promise you that she will be your wife within three days.

EUTROPE.

I desire nothing more, and, thanks to you, I'm filled with joy. But, above all, I beg you to handle this matter gently; I would be distressed if she were treated poorly as a result of this.

HILAIRE.

Now relax; you'll hear from me soon; I need to find out more about all of this. Whoa, coachman! Morille!

SCENE III.

HILAIRE, MORILLE.

MORILLE.

How may I be of service, sir? Should I harness the horses to the carriage? They are in good shape. I can say without bragging that in all of Paris there is no coachman who takes better care of his horses as I; I have just brought them from the blacksmith.

HILAIRE.

Why did you take them to the blacksmith?

MORILLE.

There was one, sir, which broke a shoe while coming back from the watering trough and another one was missing five or six nails.

HILAIRE.

You seem to get along well enough with the blacksmith to eat horseshoes and nails with him.

MORILLE.

I am not one of those scoundrels, you must not know me. I know that most of the coachmen drink with the saddle maker, the blacksmith, and the wheelwright; but I have no interest in that.

HILAIRE.

I believe that you are more responsible than the others.
Tell me about the young man who meets my niece and
walks with her and who yesterday, in the Bois de
Vincennes, walked hand in hand with her in secluded
areas.

MORILLE.

I don't know what you mean, sir.

HILAIRE.

How can you not know what I mean?

MORILLE.

I don't know what you mean.

HILAIRE.

Do you mean to say that it isn't true?

MORILLE.

Me, sir, I don't mean anything.

HILAIRE.

You have obviously been paid to be discreet, but you must
tell me the truth.

MORILLE.

I am.

HILAIRE.

What are you telling me?

MORILLE.

I'm telling you that I don't know anything about it.

HILAIRE.

How dare you lie with such impertinence?

MORILLE.

I'm not lying.

HILAIRE.

You aren't lying? You scoundrel! I saw this with my own eyes.

MORILLE *embarrassed.*

You saw it all yourself; because… as for me… I didn't see anything. (*Aside.*) What do I do now?

HILAIRE.

Do you have the audacity to tell me that you saw nothing? Hmm? Answer! Speak!

MORILLE.

Sir, I'd rather keep quiet than to speak ill of it.

HILAIRE.

Don't think that you'll be saved by your silence; I want you to talk.

MORILLE.

But if speaking about it, what am I to say?

HILAIRE.

You must tell me what you know.

MORILLE.

I don't know anything.

HILAIRE.

What! You persist in denying it? You'll be damned…

MORILLE *aside*.

I'll have to pay the piper. (*Aloud.*) Do I worry about what a master or mistress does? I think only about driving my carriage and what my orders are.

HILAIRE.

I absolutely want to know who this man is with whom she is having an affair.

MORILLE.

Sir, a servant does not stick his nose in the affairs of those who pay him, unless they allow it.

HILAIRE.

Well, I demand that you tell me. Who is the gentleman having a relationship with my niece?

MORILLE.

It is not for servants to ponder the actions of those they serve.

HILAIRE.

Will you answer my question?

MORILLE.

I'm not in the mood.

HILAIRE.

I'm losing my patience.

MORILLE.

In the two months that I have served you, I didn't think that you'd ever complain about what I have to say.

HILAIRE.

Go to Hell!

MORILLE.

Well, we know how to watch what we say.

HILAIRE.

I hope that you die of the plague!

MORILLE.

You probably want to test me, but you don't control me.

HILAIRE.

May the Heavens confound you!

MORILLE.

I'm not one of those people who allow themselves to talk indiscriminately about their masters.

HILAIRE.

May a thunderbolt crush you!

MORILLE.

We know how to live, thank God.

HILAIRE.

Oh! I can't take anymore!

MORILLE.

In my world, it's necessary to see everything, to hear everything, and to keep quiet.

HILAIRE.

You rascal! I'll...

MORILLE.

It is the maxim of the great men.

HILAIRE.

Uhhh! I hate this.

MORILLE.

Although I'm only a coachman, I have morals, and I can say, without arrogance, that I've seen, read and accepted, and that...

HILAIRE.

Ah, assassin! I want to strangle you.

MORILLE.

Gently, gently, sir, you are getting angry.

HILAIRE.

Eh! Am I not right about it, dog that you are?

MORILLE.

Sir, stay calm and listen to me with good grace.

HILAIRE.

What do you want to say to me?

MORILLE.

Are we unjust? Would you want me to inform your niece of the affair you have been having with a certain bourgeois lady? A lady that I discretely bring to you, twice a week, by the backdoor, and I lead, by your orders, to the cloak room? Would you want that?

HILAIRE.

That is not the issue at hand.

MORILLE.

True, but it is to make you recognize that a servant should be discrete, and that he should never question that which concerns his superiors.

HILAIRE.

Is that all you have to tell me? Am I to get no other information from you?

MORILLE.

Would you find it agreeable if, after having honored me with your confidence, I went blabbing recklessly about your little affair, and…

HILAIRE *slapping him.*

Damn you! This is just too much.

MORILLE.

You are wrong, sir, and you should see that I am right.

HILAIRE.

And you felt my answer to that.

MORILLE.

Your answer was violent, and I won't suffer it. (*Aside.*) What a burden my master's love is!

HILAIRE.

Someone is coming! I'll have to find out another way.

SCENE IV.

HILAIRE, MORILLE, ROLINE.

ROLINE.

What do you want, sir?

HILAIRE.

Have my niece brought in!

ROLINE.

She is busy, sir.

HILAIRE.

Doing what?

ROLINE.

She is beating her young lackey.

HILAIRE.

She can beat him another time. Have her brought in now.

ROLINE.

Must I come as well, sir?

HILAIRE.

No, I won't need you.

SCENE V.

HILAIRE, MORILLE.

MORILLE *softly*.

I fear that the niece...

HILAIRE.

About what are you mumbling?

MORILLE.

I was saying, sir, I don't like the way you are behaving and I will not work for you much longer.

HILAIRE.

You scoundrel, what if I take a stick...

MORILLE *wanting to get away*.

Oh! Take whatever you want.

HILAIRE *grabbing him.*

Where do you think you're going?

MORILLE.

I'm going to tend to my horses; they are calling me.

HILAIRE.

Your horses don't need you. Stay here!

MORILLE.

I will, but if you hit me again, I'll leave immediately.

SCENE VI.

HILAIRE, DOROTHÉE, MORILLE.

DOROTHÉE.

I was told that you were asking for me, uncle.

HILAIRE.

Yes, come here. Who is the gentleman who has been meeting you during your walks, and with whom you were in deep conversation yesterday in the Bois de Vincennes?

DOROTHÉE.

Me, uncle?

HILAIRE.

Yes, you.

DOROTHÉE.

Has Morille has been spreading lies to you?

MORILLE.

Me? I have done no such thing! An hour ago, I was beaten in an attempt to make me to talk about things of which I have no knowledge, but I remained honorable.

HILAIRE *to Morille.*

Shut up! (*To Dorothée.*) What is your answer?

DOROTHÉE *reassuring.*

Uncle, I don't know about whom you are speaking, I must have been mistaken for someone else.

HILAIRE.

It is useless to deny the truth; I saw it.

DOROTHÉE.

Uhhh! I don't have an answer uncle.

HILAIRE.

Do you admit that it's true?

DOROTHÉE.

No, uncle, please: I'll tell you only that I can't convince you, and that even if there were any truth to the rumors, I would always submit to your will.

HILAIRE.

Well! That is some escape through the quagmire. Listen, niece, you know that you have been promised to Mr. Eutrope, a man who loves you, and, what is more, he has the right, should he chose, to sue us for breach of contract which would cost us more than ten thousand *écus*[5] if we lost to him. So prepare yourself to marry him.

DOROTHÉE.

Whatever pleases you uncle.

HILAIRE.

Well said! However, until your wedding, I forbid you to leave home without my consent. *(To Morille.)* And you are forbidden to harness the horses without my permission.

SCENE VII.

DOROTHÉE, MORILLE.

DOROTHÉE.

Well, Morille, what do you think of all this?

MORILLE.

What can I say, ma'am, other than that your lovers and those of my Master are in a very bad situation?

DOROTHÉE.

What can we do to rectify the situation, Morille?

MORILLE.

I have no idea. Which character should I be now? You wanted meetings with my master, and so I was sent here as a coachman, even though I have never driven a coach in my life. I hope you realize how lucky it is that my inexperience hasn't caused a broken neck or limb. I don't know if I can play another role without your uncle's notice.

DOROTHÉE.

But, Morille, is it all hopeless?

MORILLE.

Damn! There is so much role playing, and it's you who must address it. I'm asking you to let me go. To serve you lovers, I have performed the job of coachman despite myself. It pulls me like malignant magnet. Frankly, I fear that I may suffer the fate of Mr. Phaëton[6] and that thunder may strike me. It is a reminder that your uncle has already slapped me as hard as Jupiter across on my face.

DOROTHÉE.

I'm sorry, but to ease your unhappiness, take this ring, but don't desert me like this.

MORILLE.

I must go to my master to warn him of what is happening.

DOROTHÉE.

Make sure that I can talk to him.

MORILLE.

But where, ma'am?

DOROTHÉE.

I don't know.

MORILLE.

Nor do I: unless you let me bring him to the house.

DOROTHÉE *leaving.*

Just do as you are told!

SCENE VIII.

MORILLE *alone.*

I have had enough, just enough. This ring can, in some ways, compensate me for the pain of a slap in the face and… but I must not lose any time, I will go right now to look for my master.

Exits.

SCENE IX.

JULIE, ROSETTE, ADRIAN.

ROSETTE *coming out.*

Ma'am, look; I think that's Morille. Yes, that is him, call him.

JULIE.

Shush; I don't want Lisidor to know that I'm in this city.

ROSETTE.

Maybe if I talked to Morille…

JULIE.

Do as I say and nothing more.

ADRIAN.

Ma'am, this is Mr. Hilaire's home, as I have told you, it is his niece with whom Mr. Lisidor is passionately in love.

JULIE.

Traitor! Unfaithful man!

ADRIAN.

You sent me here a month ago to watch how your lover behaved. I wasted no time, and the letters that I sent you were an accurate record.

JULIE.

Trust me, I'm happy with what you have done and that you have been here for me.

ADRIAN.

Ma'am, I am your loyal servant. What did you think of the note that I sent to Mr. Eutrope? It should bring this to a head so that he might catch your lover with this woman.

JULIE.

Nothing was better conceived, and it was skillfully done.

ROSETTE.

I told you, ma'am, my brother knew about it long ago and he was no fool: he's a partner in crime. Although he is not any richer than I, he is money-minded; he has an income of more than five hundred *écus*. Gambling has provided a large part of it, as have other little situations that present themselves. He earns the rest. I admit that while there aren't often many good characters in all of this, this must be excused; he has a lot in common with lords who are far greater than he.

ADRIAN.

My sister likes to joke.

ROSETTE.

I like to speak frankly and without exaggeration; so tell me why this home has a coachman, Morille, who has never driven a carriage.

ADRIAN.

As I told you ma'am, this was surely a ploy to aid in their meetings. During all of the walks, I noticed that Mr. Lisidor was always somewhere around.

ROSETTE.

That's true; pardon my short memory.

JULIE.

Leave us, Adrian, take my clothes to the inn, and no matter what, do not let anyone know who I am.

ADRIAN.

Do not worry ma'am!

SCENE X.

JULIE, ROSETTE.

ROSETTE.

You are in such a state ma'am, how do you want to handle this?

JULIE.

Alas, dear Rosette, the state of my soul is in much more disarray than my body. Why must I love a man who is so unfaithful?

ROSETTE.

True, Mr. Lisidor is not honoring his responsibilities at all; he is hardly a gentleman. But this is the typical of all unfaithful men.

JULIE.

Why can't I change like that?

ROSETTE.

You should forget this capricious man!

JULIE.

He is capricious, but, Rosette, I love him.

ROSETTE.

He doesn't deserve for you to even think of him! The promise of marriage that he offered you is quite serious but now he is trying to make you lose faith. Banish this fickle man from your mind. You must rule over him in his deceit. He must be a very bad man: when I think of the passionate words he so often used to express his feelings for you, I lose all sense of myself. As for me, I have told you everything he has said, I had put as much faith in him as you, and I even felt in my heart… stirrings… which spread all over, and which inspired… desires…. In truth, ma'am, he is an evil man. *Julie laughs.* You laugh, and that's something; but, for the life of me, I would have my revenge.

JULIE.

And what would you do?

ROSETTE.

I'd marry another man right under his nose.

JULIE.

Ah, Rosette! When we love so much, it isn't in our power to do what you say.

ROSETTE.

Personally, I would give him no second chances. You love someone else? Farewell, go to hell.

JULIE.

You seem very happy, Rosette, to abandon your passions so easily.

ROSETTE.

With a little willpower those feelings will come to an end.

JULIE.

Yet, you have not entirely forgotten Morille.

ROSETTE.

What a bunch of muck! I don't think about him anymore.

JULIE.

However, when you saw him, you could not stop yourself from showing a lot of emotion; it was written all over your face.

ROSETTE.

I don't deny it; you know that when you have had a friendship, and you see the person whom you loved, it's difficult not to feel some small stirrings... in the heart... which... Wouldn't you feel comfortable talking to Mr. Lisidor?

JULIE.

I'd be delighted to see him; but I'd be angry that he had seen me.

ROSETTE.

But, ma'am, what is your plan?

JULIE.

I don't know yet, Rosette; but time will provide me with the means to triumph over my fickle lover, and...

SCENE XI.

ADRIAN, JULIE, ROSETTE.

ADRIAN *returning*.

Ma'am, along my way, I ran into Morille and Mr. Lisidor, they are probably coming here; I ran here to warn you.

JULIE.

Let's move away from here, and try to watch them.

SCENE XII.

MORILLE, LISIDOR; JULIE, ROSETTE, ADRIAN
hiding.

MORILLE.

Sir, stay here and be patient, I will carefully try to find a way to get you into the house and into my quarters.

LISIDOR.

Go, Morille, and hurry back, I can hardly wait to talk to my dear Dorothée. I hope that once we are together we will find a way to around the problems that threaten us. I will risk everything for the joy of becoming her husband. But wait, I think I see someone coming, let's move away.

SCENE XIII.

EUTROPE *alone.*

Love! It rules my heart for Dorothée! When I don't see her, I'm worried sick, and when I see her, I feel an indescribable joy. I can't wait to see her and to see if Mr. Hilaire has had any success with his plans regarding the information I shared earlier. I must go in!

He knocks on Mr. Hilaire's door.

SCENE XIV.

EUTROPE, ROLINE.

ROLINE.

How may I help you, sir?

EUTROPE.

Is Mr. Hilaire at home?

ROLINE.

No, sir.

EUTROPE.

And Miss Dorothée?

ROLINE.

She is in her room: come, I'll take you there.

EUTROPE.

Thank you!

SCENE XV.

LISIDOR *returning.*

I'm despondent! Did my damned rival have to show up at this very moment to halt our plan? But, no matter; so long as, whatever happens, I talk to my darling Dorothée.

SCENE XVI.

LISIDOR, MORILLE; JULIE, ROSETTE, ADRIAN *hiding.*

MORILLE.

Everything is ready for you to come to my shabby room. Come soon, and when I have a chance, I'll handle the rest.

LISIDOR.

But...

MORILLE.

No buts; follow me!

SCENE XVII.

JULIE, ROSETTE AND ADRIAN *coming out from where they were hiding.*

ADRIAN.

Well! ma'am, you can no longer deny it.

JULIE.

Oh, heaven! I can't believe what have I just seen and heard! That traitor!

ROSETTE.

Ma'am, you must go in there and beat the devil out of that cheater and his valet.

JULIE.

That coward! That scoundrel! Adrian, go to the house and do as I told you.

ADRIAN.

Of course, ma'am.

Exits.

SCENE XVIII.

JULIE, ROSETTE.

JULIE.

The cheat! To betray me this way!

ROSETTE.

Frankly, I would have already set fire to the house

JULIE.

Cunning will be more effective than violence here.

ROSETTE.

At least he would remember the violence. But what do you plan to do? Personally, I want to hurt him. Oh, how I'd love to punch the two-timer and make him buckle under his own betrayal and his fickleness.

JULIE *after a little reflection.*

Stop with these outbursts, raise your hood, go straight in, and ask for the master of the house.

ROSETTE.

Why, ma'am?

JULIE.

No questions let me do what I must.

ROSETTE.

But if I see Morille, the first thing I'll do is box his ears.

JULIE.

No, I forbid it; you'll ruin my plan. Don't move; I'll go there myself, but most importantly, don't speak.

ROSETTE *raising her hood.*

I'll try to show some control.

SCENE XIX.

HILAIRE; JULIE, ROSETTE *who have raised their hoods. As Julie moves forward, she bumps into Hilaire, who is exiting with his skeleton key.*

HILAIRE.

For what are you looking, ma'am?

JULIE *her hood raised.*

I'm looking for Mr. Hilaire, the master of this house.

HILAIRE.

You are speaking to him, ma'am.

JULIE *kneeling.*

Ah, then sir, allow me to beg for your justice.

HILAIRE *helping her up.*

Against whom, ma'am?

JULIE.

Against a treacherous traitor, a villain in your house.

HILAIRE.

And who is that?

JULIE.

It's Morille, sir, your coachman.

HILAIRE.

And what did he do to you?

JULIE.

Alas! You mean what hasn't he done? He has left me desolate with two poor, small children.

HILAIRE.

What! Are you his wife?

JULIE.

Yes, sir, much to my sorrow.

HILAIRE.

He did not tell me that he was married, but most of my servants keep their affairs private to maintain their situations. Anyway, what do you need from me?

JULIE.

I would only like to see him. Would you be so kind as to let me speak to him?

HILAIRE.

Gladly, but let me see your face.

JULIE *lowering her hood.*

Certainly.

HILAIRE.

Good Heavens but you are lovely! You are the wife of that scoundrel?

JULIE.

Yes, sir, since Heaven decreed it.

HILAIRE.

It is a shame that you are the wife of such a smug scoundrel

JULIE.

He is my husband.

HILAIRE.

He is not worthy of that title, and you deserve better.

JULIE.

You flatter me, sir.

35

HILAIRE.

I'd be pleased to take your part against him, and, thus, show the high regard that I hold for you.

JULIE.

I would be indebted to you!

HILAIRE.

Your plight has so touched me that I'd strangle him if he refused to do his duty to you.

JULIE.

I'm very grateful!

HILAIRE.

Not at all; on the contrary, it is I, by serving you, who will be indebted to you. A woman as beautiful and fine as you assuredly deserves some kindness shown to her. That rascal! Who is this lady with you?

JULIE.

She is my cousin. (*To Rosette*). Greet the gentleman!

ROSETTE *lowering her hood.*

I'm your very humble servant.

HILAIRE.

She is rather pretty, but, frankly, not as pretty as you. I'm going to open my apartment for you, and there we will speak to him bluntly.

SCENE XX.

JULIE, ROSETTE.

ROSETTE.

Oh my, ma'am, I think that Mr. Hilaire feels moved… in him… something for you.

JULIE.

Who cares?

ROSETTE.

He takes great interest in your welfare and with much warmth, and that means you evoke feelings in him which… Well, you know.

JULIE.

I really don't care; but I'm very glad that he is supporting me in this situation.

ROSETTE.

You are not doing anything wrong; but, please, ma'am, what's the point in saying that you are Morille's wife? I don't understand.

JULIE.

Don't be jealous; it's to better control things and to avoid committing an unfaithful act.

ROSETTE.

You show such concern for a lover who is betraying you.

JULIE.

That's true; but love…

ROSETTE.

But love… but love… love is a fool, when it forgives a cheater. As for me, I won't die satisfied until I've knocked him out.

JULIE.

Your aggressive nature always goes to the extreme. But let me handle this, and don't speak unless I say so.

ROSETTE.

I understand and I will obey you.

JULIE.

The doors are opening, let's raise our hoods.

SCENE XXI.

(The door is pulled shut.)

HILAIRE, ROLINE, JULIE, ROSETTE.

ROLINE *to Hilaire.*

Mr. Eutrope is upstairs with your niece, sir.

HILAIRE.

I'm glad. Go on, Roline, and have Morille brought to me.

ROLINE *bowing.*

Do you need anything else, sir?

HILAIRE.

No, leave and do as you are told.

ROLINE *leaving.*

Immediately, sir!

HILAIRE *to Julie.*

Ma'am, this will be your servant's room. You are in charge.

JULIE.

Oh! Mister…

HILAIRE.

Morille is coming; go into this room to listen to us so you can see how I handle this situation.

JULIE *leaving the* room.

Okay.

Rosette also leaves the room.

SCENE XXII.

HILAIRE, MORILLE; JULIE, ROSETTE *hiding.*

MORILLE.

How may I be service, sir?

HILAIRE.

Come here, you rascal; you scoundrel. Aren't you ashamed of what you are doing?

MORILLE.

Me, sir?

HILAIRE.

Yes, you; of course, you!

MORILLE.

And what am I doing, sir?

HILAIRE.

What are you doing? You traitor!

MORILLE *softly*.

I'm shaking. I don't understand what you mean.

HILAIRE.

I mean that you are a foolish reprobate, and you deserve severe punishment to teach you a lesson.

MORILLE *aside*.

The jig is up.

HILAIRE.

Well, atone for your wrongdoing, and tell me the truth.

MORILLE.

I'll do whatever you want. (*Aside.*) Is he out of his mind?

HILAIRE.

To betray a person for whom you should have the greatest respect! What causes such treachery?

MORILLE *softly*.

Everything has been discovered. (*Aloud.*)

HILAIRE.

What? Speak up!

MORILLE.

Sir… Sir…

HILAIRE.

Well, what?

MORILLE *kneeling.*

I beg for your forgiveness.

HILAIRE *bringing Julie in from the room.*

It is not my forgiveness you should seek, but rather that of the person who, with your shameful ways, has been most foully mistreated.

MORILLE.

Oh, good Heavens! What is this? Where am I?

HILAIRE.

There you are, scoundrel! Come on, let's embrace all that was said to me earlier; let's see your remorse, and let's beg her to find forgiveness in her heart for you. (*To Julie.*) Would you like to?

JULIE *to Hilaire.*

Anything to please you, sir.

HILAIRE *to Morille.*

Oh, you rascal, you don't deserve such a lovely lady. Come on then, kiss her!

MORILLE *resisting.*

Uh! Sir!

HILAIRE.

What! You are showing disgust!

JULIE.

You see, sir.

HILAIRE *taking ahold of Morille's arm.*

Quickly; do as I say!

MORILLE *pulling back.*

Are you kidding me, sir?

HILAIRE.

Am I kidding you that I want you to reconcile with your wife?

MORILLE.

My wife?

HILAIRE.

Yes, your wife with whom you have two small children.

MORILLE.

Me?

HILAIRE.

Yes, you; do you dare to claim that you are not married to her?

MORILLE.

Yes, sir, I dare since I am not.

JULIE *to Morille.*

This is shameful! How can you say this without blushing?

MORILLE.

What? That you are not my wife?

JULIE.

Yes! I am; your indulgences have taken you away from me to another woman, who is probably is worth less than I. My home, Le Mans, bears witness to what I say.

HILAIRE.

Our debaucheries often lead us to abandon lovely women and chase after wenches and well-coiffed goats.

JULIE *to Hilaire.*

What would I gain by coming here and calling myself his wife if he were not my husband?

HILAIRE.

Indeed! What do you have to say about that? To her, you're just source of money.

MORILLE *aside.*

I don't know anything about anything.

HILAIRE.

Well, what do you have to say to that?

MORILLE.

Sir… If she wants to be my wife, I'm okay with that.

HILAIRE.

Really, you are very sick! He is to be pitied! Come on, kiss her now!

MORILLIE *going to kiss her.*

As you wish, sir and with all of my heart.

JULIE.

No, sir; allow me not to; he has refused me in your presence, and it's only fitting that I refuse him so he may earn that reward.

HILAIRE.

By damn, she's right! I wouldn't do anything less in her place. (*To Julie.*) But for my sake, offer your hand to him.

JULIE *presenting her hand to Morille.*

I obey your wishes with pleasure.

MORILLE *kissing her hand, and Julie pulling her hand back.*

Me too.

HILAIRE *holding Julie's hand.*

I'm pleased to see you on good terms and to know that I helped.

JULIE.

I thank you from the bottom of my heart.

MORILLE.

Sir, I am your servant. (*Aside.*) I really don't follow this.

HILAIRE *to Julie.*

There, that wasn't so bad; you must properly cement this reconciliation by staying in my home with your husband. My niece is getting married in the next three days, and I need, in her absence, a person who will care for my house; I'd be delighted to place the operation in your hands. What do you say?

JULIE.

I'll do all that you wish.

HILAIRE *to Morille.*

And you, what do you say?

MORILLE.

I don't object to the idea. (*Aside.*) I just don't understand any of this.

HILAIRE.

Your reunion will not be complete until you sleep together.

MORILLE *aside.*

I'd like to see that.

JULIE.

There is no hurry, sir.

HILAIRE.

I agree; but, in these kinds of reunions, the individual man and woman are in need of help to overcome many challenges. You can, for now, have this room, get undressed, and go to bed!

JULIE.

Uh! Sir...

MORILLE *getting undressed.*

As for me, sir, I'm ready to obey.

HILAIRE to *Morille.*

It is done; (*To Julie.*) You should follow his lead and show a little enthusiasm.

JULIE.

Sir, let me...

HILAIRE.

No, you must be in bed together, I will leave you with your husband; this will seal what I have begun.

JULIE.

I'm confused by your kindness.

HILAIRE *to Morille.*

She is charming!

MORILLE.

That is true.

HILAIRE.

Go do you duty, and I'll hear no complaints

MORILLE.

I will. (*Aside.*) My Lord, this is strange, let's see where this leads.

HILAIRE *to Julie.*

I'm looking for your complete satisfaction.

JULIE.

I'll fulfil these last obligations. So thank you, sir, for all of the kindness that you have bestowed upon us.

HILAIRE.

I'll leave you. You must excuse him, he is confounded.

MORILLE.

Another man would do less. (*Aside.*) My master plagues me! (*Aloud.*) Sir, my excessive silence is evidence of… my… extreme… gratitude.

HILAIRE *to Morille.*

That is well said. I'm going to leave you with that thought and go to another room. A third person is always inconvenient in such situations.

JULIE *to Hilaire.*

Allow her to stay a moment here, and then she will leave.

HILAIRE.

You have your reasons, and I won't interfere. Morille will get her settled in with Roline. Be assured of my regard!

JULIE.

It would be a mistake to doubt it.

SCENE XXIII.

JULIE, MORILLE

JULIE *after having closed the door.*

Here we are as I had hoped. Come now, Mr. Rogue, what
do you have to say?

SCENE XXIV.

ROSETTE, JULIE, MORILLE.

ROSETTE *appearing.*

So this is how we find you, rascal.

MORILLE.

What, Rosette too?

ROSETTE.

Yes, it's Rosette, you fraud; but answer Madame.

MORILLE *to Rosette.*

How do you want me to answer her? She said that she
was my wife; she has children by me; all of Le Mans knows
it; I don't understand what she is doing.

JULIE.

I want to thwart your scheme and force you to explain the deceit of your master to me.

MORILLE *to Julie.*

I'm not a fraud. Has Mr. Hilaire upset you?

JULIE.

I'm not talking about Mr. Hilaire; it's the traitor Lisidor, you mongrel.

MORILLE.

Ma'am, I have neither been with him nor seen him in three months.

JULIE.

You shameless liar! Isn't he in love with Mr. Hilaire's niece? And don't you drive him to see his new love?

MORILLE.

That's not true.

ROSETTE *slapping him.*

Disrespectful reprobate! A liar deserves to be slapped; we know what you're up to.

MORILLE *to Rosette.*

I don't understand your rage.

ROSETTE.

Oh, you don't; you deserve another one. So answer her, answer, and tell her the truth because every time you lie, you'll be slapped.

JULIE.

Where is Lisidor?

MORILLE *wanting to take leave.*

He is wherever he wants to be; it's none of my business.

JULIE *stopping him from leaving.*

No, no, you must not go.

MORILLE *resisting.*

Ma'am, let me go.

JULIE.

Oh, you scoundrel! I ought to strangle you.

ROSETTE.

Let's beat this schemer. You traitor! You villain! You'll feel our fists.

MORILLE *yelling.*

Help! Murder! Ah! Ah! I'm being beaten.

SCENE XXV.

HILAIRE, JULIE, ROSETTE, MORILLE.

HILAIRE *from the other side of the door.*

What is the racket in there?

JULIE *after having opened the door.*

Sir, this evil man is trying to kill me and without reason. I think that he has crippled me.

HILAIRE *pushing him roughly.*

How vile! How dare you assault your wife under my roof! Oh! I'll teach you something.

ROSETTE *to Hilaire.*

Sir, he hit me. I think that I have a broken neck. Uhhh! I can't take this anymore.

MORILLE *to Hilaire.*

Sir, they are not telling the truth, and I'll tell you...

HILAIRE *pushing him.*

Shut up, wretch, shut up; otherwise I'll treat you the way that you deserve. *(To Julie.)* Your concerns are important to me. *(To Morille.)* Now, go to your stable, and leave us here.

JULIE, *getting in front of Morille, to Hilaire.*

No, sir, I'll not allow him to leave; he will run from here.

HILAIRE *to Julie.*

What?

JULIE.

You must be told of his deception; I can hide it no longer. Just half an hour ago, he hid a man here. He is probably still here; you must find out what it's all about.

HILAIRE.

What are you saying?

JULIE.

I'm telling you the truth; we saw him.

ROSETTE.

Nothing is more certain, sir, and that's what we were fighting about when he began hitting us.

HILAIRE.

There may be some truth in what you are saying; it's probably a certain gentleman, who, they say, wants my niece, and who, possibly, has information on him. (*To Morille.*) Who is this man?

MORILLE *embarrassed.*

Sir... I don't know...

HILAIRE.

It will be your death! Your life! I want to know, or I will ruin you.

MORILLE.

Sir, I beg your forgiveness. He is one of my friends, a very gallant man, who fears arrest for an honorable act, and who, for his safety, begged me to hide him for two or three days in my quarters.

HILAIRE.

What? Without my permission?

MORILLE.

Forgive me; I didn't have the time to discuss it with you.

JULIE.

Trust me, sir! He is manipulating you; the kindness that you have shown me forces me to take your side over his.

HILAIRE *caressing her.*

You don't need to explain!

JULIE.

If you want me to tell you more, have this man brought to me and, before them all, I will tell you everything.

HILAIRE.

Anything to please you! (*To Morille.*) I'm beginning to believe that you're an impostor. Give me the key!

MORILLE.

I'll go with you, sir.

HILAIRE.

I don't want you to. Stay here!

JULIE.

You can't let this man leave and for good reason.

(*Morille gives his key to Hilaire.*)

HILAIRE *leaving, to Julie.*

Leave it to me; you will not be displeased!

SCENE XXVI.

JULIE, ROSETTE, MORILLE.

ROSETTE *to Morille.*

Well, Mr. Rogue, all of your deceptions will end soon.

MORILLE *to Rosette.*

What do you want me to do? This isn't my fault.

ROSETTE.

Who else then, you mongrel?

MORILLE.

I was forced to do what I have done by the violent behavior of my master. My dear Rosette, am I not worthy of the forgiveness I seek? (*To Julie.*) Ma'am, I'm lost, have mercy on me.

ROSETTE.

You will play the sleeping dog now.

MORILLE.

Rosette, my dear Rosette, for the love I have for you, help me to be forgiven, somehow, damn it. I'm not guilty.

ROSETTE *to Julie.*

Ma'am, he is speaking with an open heart.

JULIE *to Rosette.*

Do you think that he is telling the truth?

MORILLE.

This plague will choke me, or the Devil will get me.

ROSETTE *to Morille.*

Do you think that we'll believe what you swear is the truth?

MORILLE.

What, Rosette! Will you not be a rock for Morille? Don't you have any compassion for my tears, and aren't we in some way connected? Rosette, Rosette!

ROSETTE *to Julie.*

Ma'am, his tears pierce my soul, I beg you to forgive him.

JULIE.

Well, I forgive him on your part.

MORILLE.

Oh! I'm so happy now! No matter what happens now, I have your support. That is enough.

ROSETTE *to Morille.*

On my life, don't lie to me again; otherwise…

MORILLE *embracing her.*

Rosette, believe me that I was in great despair for having made you unhappy, and when he goes to the gallows…

SCENE XXVII.

DOROTHÉE, JULIE, MORILLE, ROSETTE.

DOROTHÉE *behind the scene.*

Morille!

MORILLE *meeting Dorothée.*

Shall we? This is Dorothée.

JULIE *to Rosette.*

Let's be quiet!

DOROTHÉE *entering.*

What is that sound I hear?

MORILLE *to Dorothée.*

I don't know.

DOROTHÉE *to Morille.*

Who are these ladies?

MORILLE.

I don't know.

DOROTHÉE.

Why are they here?

MORILLE.

I don't know.

DOROTHÉE.

What do they want?

MORILLE.

Your uncle.

DOROTHÉE.

My uncle? Where is he?

MORILLE.

He'll be here soon with Mr. Lisidor.

DOROTHÉE.

What are you saying?

MORILLE.

I'm saying that everything has been discovered.

DOROTHÉE.

What?

MORILLE.

Here they come.

DOROTHÉE *aside.*

Dear Heaven, I am unhappy!

SCENE XXVIII.

HILAIRE, LISIDOR, JULIE, DOROTHÉE, MORILLE, ROSETTE.

HILAIRE *to Lisidor.*

Sir, now you must explain everything clearly and plainly.

LISIDOR *aside.*

Whom do I see? Is Julie here?

HILAIRE.

Okay, now tell me, why are you in my house? Answer!

LISIDOR, *embarrassed, to Hilaire.*

Sir, this is not the place to explain things. When we are alone, I will tell you everything.

HILAIRE.

We needn't be alone for that; now you must speak frankly.

LISIDOR.

If that is how you want it, then I will do nothing that you ask, sir.

JULIE *to Lisidor, stopping him.*

No, you are not leaving, not until I've cleared up everything.

LISIDOR *to Julie.*

Ma'am...

JULIE.

"Ma'am":[7] Well, what do you have to say?

HILAIRE *to Julie.*

What is this?

JULIE *to Hilaire.*

You must understand sir, that much to my sorrow, I love this rogue, and he has promised to marry me. He is, however, breaking his word to me and trying to ensnare your niece.

HILAIRE.

You have a promise of marriage from this gentleman?

JULIE.

Yes, sir, and here it is.

HILAIRE.

So you aren't Morille's wife?

JULIE.

No, sir, and Morille is my unfaithful fiancé's servant.

ROSETTE.

It is the whole truth, sir, and I am Madame's servant. Well tell him, isn't that the truth?

HILAIRE *to Morille.*

How do you answer that, you rogue?

MORILLE *to Hilaire.*

Umm... I have nothing, sir.

HILAIRE *to Lisidor.*

I understand. Enough is enough. And you, sir, what do you have to say about all of this?

LISIDOR.

Maybe it's true; maybe it isn't.

HILAIRE.

Your answer is that of someone from Normandy.[8] (*To Dorothée.*) And you, my niece, what do you have to say about all of this?

DOROTHÉE *taking leave*.

He's a rogue and a villain! I hate him.

SCENE XXIX

HILAIRE, LISIDOR, JULIE, ROSETTE, MORILLE.

HILAIRE *to Lisidor and Morille*.

Very well! Damn it, if you don't get out of my house immediately, I'll turn you in as liars and kidnappers!

JULIE.

Sir, please forgive the liberties that I've taken, and pardon the tenderness of a jealous lover…

HILAIRE.

Go to Hell, and get out of my house now! As for my niece, she'll marry Mr. Eutrope tomorrow or go to a convent. (*To Morille, giving him a slap, and taking leave.*) And for you, that's your salary.

FINAL SCENE.

LISIDOR, JULIE, ROSETTE, MORILLE.

MORILLE.

And this is how I am paid my wages.

ROSETTE.

You worked cheaply.

LISIDOR *to Julie.*

I know all too well, that I am liable for what I've done to you; but I am prepared to do whatever you ask, if only you will grant me the forgiveness I seek. (*Getting on his knees.*)

JULIE *lifting him up.*

It is too easy to forgive those we love.

MORILLE.

And you, Rosette, won't you do the same for me?

ROSETTE.

With all of my heart.

LISIDOR.

But what has brought you here?

JULIE.

You'll learn later. Let's go, and not give Mr. Hilaire more reason to complain.

MORILLE.

I'm with you; it certainly isn't smart for me to stay here.

THE END.

NOTES TO PREFACE

[1] Brécourt's play was the last before his death in 1685. As a comedy on Lucian of Samosata's *Timon the Misanthrope*, it should not be a surprise to Lancaster that the play "is surprisingly gloomy for a one-act comedy" (IV^2, p. 511). What is surprising, and perhaps due in part to Brécourt's flamboyant personality, is its strong success.

[2] See Curtis (1972), p. 57.

[3] Antonio Hurtado de Mendoza, *Los Riesgos que tiene un coche* (1653). Hauteroche writes, in the *Avis* that the "l'idée du sujet" came to him from Mendoza, but that he "l'a fort dépaïsée." Lancaster (IV^2, p. 515).

[4] Lucette (II, vii) assails Pourceaugnac with a case of abandonment and also of paternity, all in a heavy southern (Pézenas) accent.

NOTES TO TEXT

[1.] Hauteroche's working title for the play was *Le Cocher supposé* (*The Supposed Coachman*). Before its production he changed the title to *Le Cocher* (*The Coachman*). This is, in my opinion, a better title because the audience cannot be sure until the last third of the play whether Morille is a coachman or a supposed coachman. After Hauteroche's death the play has often been published and performed as *Le Cocher supposé*.

[2.] Le Mans is a city in France, located on the Sarthe River. It is 127 miles south-west of Paris.

[3.] Les Invalides, also known as L'Hôtel national des Invalides, was a hospital and a retirement home for war veterans. Its construction began in 1671, and it was completed in 1678.

[4.] The Bois de Vincennes is located on the eastern edge of Paris. The Château de Vincennes, a former residence of the Kings of France, is located in the Bois de Vincennes.

[5.] *Écus* are gold and silver coins, issued from the thirteenth through the eighteenth centuries, bearing the figure of a shield. See the image below:

6. In Roman mythology Jupiter is the god of the sky and of thunder. Phaëton, Jupiter's son, insisted driving the sun chariot for a day. He was, unfortunately, unable to control the horses. Since the earth was in danger of being set on fire Jupiter killed him with a thunderbolt.

7. These are my quotation marks. There are no quotation marks in the original text. Without them it might seem that Julie is calling Lisidor "Ma'am."

8. Normandy is a region approximately three hundred miles northwest of Paris. Its history has been often turbulent. In the seventeenth century its people were considered heavy drinker and rabble rousers.

CHRONOLOGY OF HAUTEROCHE'S LIFE

1617?

This is the probable year of the birth of Noël Le Breton, son of Noël I Le Breton (1598?-1678), *boutonnier*, and the mother not subsequently identified (?-1642).

1635-1637?

Hauteroche leaves Paris, with a view to a career in the army in Valencia, Spain.

He joins a French acting troupe in Valladolid.

1638-?

He directs a troupe of French actors in Germany and travels with them there.

The date of their return can't be surmised.

1650

He becomes the director of a provincial troupe that includes Catherine Desurlis, then her sisters Madeleine (1652) and Estiennette (1653). His friendship with their father Étienne Desurlis would predate their association with the troupe.

1654

Scarron creates the stock character Crispin in his comedy *L'Écolier de Salamanque.*

April 1

The *acte of association d'une troupe de comédiens de campagne sous la direction de Noël Breton, sieur de Hauteroche* is signed.

The *promesse faite par la troupe de Noël Breton, sieur de Hauteroche à Cathérine de Surlis* is signed. This is the earliest act of constitution of the troupe, for one year, co-signed by Jannequin ("Rochefort"), François de la Court, Jehan Loseu ("Beauchaisne"), Drouyn, François Serdin, and Estiennette Desurlis.

September 29

At Fontenay-le-Comte, Hauteroche becomes the godfather to the son of Claude Jannequin and Madeleine Desurlis; his troupe entertains.

1655

April

Hauteroche, now permanently with the stage name, becomes a member of the Théâtre du Marais.

1655

He remains only for the 1655-1656 season, after which the company loses its lease. The Théâtre du Marais closes from April 1657 to March 31, 1659.

Summer

He acts himself in Quinault's comedy *La Comédie sans comédie*.

1657

April

He and the members of his troupe leave Paris to act in the provinces. The exact date of their return is not known but may be within the year.

1658-59

Floridor, director of the Théâtre de l'Hôtel de Bourgogne takes on Hauteroche, as a replacement for Pierre Lazard who died in 1657.

Hauteroche's first season corresponds with Molière's return from the provinces.

1660

Molière creates *Sganarelle ou le cocu imaginaire*.

1660

March

Hauteroche's signature appears on the rental agreement of the Hôtel de Bourgogne.

1662

He creates the lead *rôle* of Baron de la Crasse in Raymond Poisson's comedy *Le Baron de la Crasse*.

He plays Pompée in Pierre Corneille's *Sertorius*.

Molière creates *L'École des femmes*.

1663

Molière creates *L'Impromptu de Versailles*, which includes a caricature of Hauteroche's tragic diction in the *rôle* of Pompée.

Hauteroche unofficially assumes on occasion Floridor's function as the *troupe*'s orateur.

March 3

Hauteroche, with the other actors, signs a four-year rental agreement on the Hôtel de Bourgogne.

1664

Fifteen lyric poems by Hauteroche appear in *Les Delices de la poesie des plus célèbres auteurs du temps*, published by Ribou and dedicated to the Pierre de Camboust, duc de Coislin.

Hauteroche's signature appears on *la lettre-mémoire* of the actors of the Hôtel de Bourgogne concerning pensions.

1665

December 18

He performs the *rôle* of Éphestion in Jean Racine's *Alexandre le grand.*

1666

January

Hauteroche performs the *rôle* of Tygrane in Thomas Corneille's *Antiochus.* This opening is a special performance for Louis XIV given by the Charles III, duc de Créqui.

1667

Hauteroche plays the *rôle* of Lira, *poète de la cour* in Jean-Baptiste Lully's *Ballet des muses.*

1667

November 19

He creates the *rôle* of Phénix in Racine's *Andromaque*.

1668

February 18

He plays, along with Brécourt, one of the *rôles* of *prétendants* in Thomas Corneille's *Laodice, reine de Cappadoce*.

June 9

Raymond Poisson's *Le Poète basque*, in which Hauteroche plays himself, is first performed.

July 12

Hauteroche's first play is produced, *L'Amant qui ne flatte point* inspired by Molière's *Le Misanthrope* (1666).

November

He creates the *rôle* of Chicanneau in Racine's comedy *Les Plaideurs*.

1669

L'Amant qui ne flatte point is first published in Paris by Guillain and de Sercy.

He plays the *rôle* of the "Coadjuteur" in Montfleury's *La Femme juge et partie* in a special performance for the duchesse de Bouillon.

February 2

He creates the *rôle* of Pompée in abbé Boyer's *Le Jeune Marius*.

February 21

He creates the *rôle* of Narcisse in Racine's *Britannicus*.

July

Hauteroche's second play *Le Soupé mal-apprêté* opens.

1670

Le Souper mal-apprêté is first published in Paris by Guillain and de Sercy.

Crispin médecin is first published by Barbin.

1670

March 22

Hauteroche signs the act of association by which Champmeslé and his wife join the Hôtel de Bourgogne.

April 25

Hauteroche signs a *mémoire* of ratification of the 1,000 *livres* pension of retired actors from the Hôtel de Bourgogne.

May 10

His third play, *Crispin médecin* opens.

November 21

He creates the *rôle* of Paulin in Racine's *Bérénice*.

1671

May 9

He creates the *rôle* of the lover Hydas in Boyer's *Atalante*.

August

After withdrawal from the theatre of the terminally ill Floridor, Hauteroche takes over directorship of the troupe and the function of *orateur*.

1671

His signature appears on the marriage contract of Claude Deschamps (de Villiers) and Jeanne Guillemain, which is also signed by his future wife Madame J-B Arnauld (Jacqueline Le Sueur) and her mother Radégonde Régnard (*née* Le Sueur).

1672

January 5

Hauteroche creates the *rôle* of Osmin in Racine's *Bajazet*.

August 6

The announcement of Hauteroche's fourth play under the title of *Les Maris infidèles ou les apparences trompeuses* is made. However, it was not produced.

November 16

He creates the lead *rôle* of Théodat in Thomas Corneille's *Théodat*.

November 24

Hauteroche's fifth play, *Le Deuil*, is first performed.

1673

Les Apparence trompeuses and *Le Deuil* are first published in
Paris by Promé. *Le Deuil* is headed by a dedication to
André Le Camus, *chevalier, conseiller ordinaire du roi.*

January 13

Hauteroche creates the *rôle* of Arbate in Racine's *Mithridate.*

January 30

Hauteroche plays in a special performance of *Mithridate*
staged as a part of the festivities of the marriage of the duc
d'Orléans and Charlotte Elisabeth de Bavière.

August 2

Crispin médecin is played for the duc d'Orléans at his request
in a private performance given for him by Monsieur de
Boisfranc at Saint-Ouen. Hauteroche is in attendance,
playing in a production of *Mithridate.*

1674

July 5

Hauteroche's sixth play, *Crispin musician* opens.

September 21

Crispin musicien is first published in Paris by Promé.

1675

Summer

This is the probable first production of his seventh play
Les Nobles de province.

September 13

His signature appears on the marriage contract of the actor
Michel Baron.

1677

January 1

He creates the *rôle* of Téramène in Racine's *Phèdre*.

1678

Hauteroche's first will and testament is drawn up, his
father appears as *légataire universel*.

Noël I Le Breton dies.

Le Deuil is performed at Versailles.

January or February

Les Nouvellistes, Hauteroche's eighth play, is first
performed. It was not published and is not extant.

1678

August 28

Les Nobles de province first published in Lyons by Amaulry, including an *Au lecteur* not subsequently published.

1679

February 15

His signature appears on the marriage contract of Jean Bouillart.

1680

March

Hauteroche's ninth play *La Bassette*, is first performed. It was not published and is not extant.

August 13

Pierre Le Breton, Hauteroche's half-brother, dies.

August 25

The merging of the Hôtel de Bourgogne and the Théâtre du Guénégaud takes place to form the single Parisian theatre known as La Comédie-Française.

1680

Hauteroche plays the *rôle* of Téramène in the opening performance of Racine's *Phèdre* at La Comédie-Française.

1682

The first collective edition of Hauteroche's plays is published by Adrien Moetjens in The Hague, *Les Pièces de théâtre du sieur de Hauteroche*, containing in order of publication *L'Amant qui ne flatte point*, *Le Soupé mal-apprêté*, *Crispin médecin*, *Le Deuil*, *Les Apparences trompeuses*, *Crispin musicien*, and *Les Nobles de province*.

Hauteroche furnishes a loan to Jacqueline Le Sueur of 2,200 *livres* for the settlement of her mother's estate.

1684

February 22

L'Esprit folet ou la dame invisible, Hauteroche's tenth play is first produced.

March 20

Hauteroche's retirement from the Hôtel de Bourgogne is officially noted by LaGrange, with *demye part à M. Raisin, l'ainé, demye à Mlle Raisin.*

1684

April 17

Hauteroche receives power of attorney for all Jacqueline Le Sueur's financial affairs.

June 7 or June 9

Le Cocher (*The Coachman*), Hauteroche's eleventh play, is first performed.

1685

L'Esprit folet ou la dame invisible and *Le Cocher* (*The Coachman*) are first published in Paris by Ribou. *Le Cocher* (*The Coachman*) has a preface not subsequently published.

June 25

Hauteroche marries Jacqueline Le Sueur. An inventory is drawn up of Jacqueline's house, rue de Beaurepaire, where the couple will reside.
August 7

Le Cocher (*The Coachman*) is performed for Louis XIV at Marly.

December 10

Hauteroche makes the loan of 3,650 *livres* to J. B. Défant, *colonel de dragons*.

1686

Hauteroche's twelfth play, *Le Feint Polonois ou la veuve impertinente* is published for the first in Lyons by Plaignard, after a probable public performance in Lyons. The play was not produced in Paris.

1687

This is the probable year of Hauteroche's blindness, from an unknown cause.

January 17

Hauteroche makes the loan of 1,600 *livres* to Anne Bellinzani, Madame Michel Ferrand.

1688

March 1

Hauteroche's signature appears on the marriage contract of the actor Duparc's son.

1689

March 22

Hauteroche and his wife rent a house on la rue Saint-Sauveur at 720 *livres* yearly.

1690

July 26-August 7

Les Bourgeoises de qualité, Hauteroche's thirteenth and last play, is produced at La Comédie-Française.

1691

Les Bourgeoises de qualité is published for the first in Paris by the veuve Gontier, who also published the second collective edition of Hauteroche's plays.

1694

Jacqueline Le Sueur's signature on the quittance for Hauteroche's pension notes his blindness and bad health.

1695

The Hauteroches rent out a house owned at 16, rue de Beaune (at 300 *livres*).

1696

A third collective edition of Hauteroche's plays is published in Paris by Guillain.

December 1

The Hauteroches sell a house owned in Aubervilliers (4,500 *livres*).

1697-1705

Hauteroche makes loans of 6,000 livres to Jean Le Roy, Greffier à la 4ᵉ Chambre des Enquêtes, and his wife Geneviève Herault, and of 20,000 *livres* to Louis Gislain, sieur de Belcourt.

1703

A fourth collective edition of Hauteroche's plays published by Ribou, containing in order of publication Crispin *musician*, Crispin *médecin*, *Le Deuil*, *Les Bourgeoises de qualité*, and *L'Esprit folet ou la dame invisible*.

1704

December 13

Hauteroche's second and final will and testament is drawn up. His executor is Louis Gislain, sieur de Belcourt. His sister Marie is *légataire universelle*.

1705

January 14

He makes a loan of 48,000 *livres* to Marie Bonneau, widow of Charles Fortier, sieur de La Hoguette.

1707

July 14

Hauteroche dies in a house on the rue de la March and is buried in the parish church of Saint-Sauveur.

1713

Jacqueline Le Sueur dies and is buried at the parish church of Saint-Suplice.

Her sister Anne-Marie Le Sueur, widow of Louis de Dours is *légataire universel*.

BIBLIOGRAPHY

HAUTEROCHE'S DRAMATIC WRITINGS

Hauteroche, Noël Le Breton. *Les Œuvres de Monsieur de Hauteroche*. La Haye: Adrian Moetjens, 1683.

_____. *Les Œuvres de Monsieur de Hauteroche*. 3 vols. Paris: Veuve de Louis Gontier, 1691.

_____. *Les Œuvres de Monsieur de Hauteroche*. 3 vols. Paris: Thomas Guillain, 1696.

_____. *Les Œuvres de Monsieur de Hauteroche*. 3 vols. Paris: Pierre-Jacques Ribou, 1703.

_____. *Les Œuvres de Monsieur de Hauteroche*. 3 vols. Paris: Pierre-Jacques Ribou, 1736.

_____. *Les Œuvres de Monsieur de Hauteroche*. 3 vols. Paris: Compagnie des Libraires Associés, 1742.

_____. *Théâtre de Noël le Breton, sieur de Hauteroche*. 3 vols. Paris: Aux Dépens de la Compagnie, 1772.

_____. *Théâtre de Hauteroche*. 3 vols. Paris: Édition Jean-Baptiste Touquet, 1821.

_____. *Chefs-d'œuvre dramatiques de Hauteroche, et Campistron*. Paris: Jules Didot, 1824.

Hauteroche. *L'Amant qui ne flatte point.* Paris: Thomas Guillain et Charles de Sercy, 1669.

_____. *L'Amant qui ne flatte point.* La Haye: Adrian Moetjens, 1682.

_____. *Le Soupé mal-apprêté.* Paris: Thomas Guillain, 1670.

_____. *Le Soupé mal apresté.* Paris: Gabriel Quinet, 1670.

_____. *Le Soupé, mal apreste.* La Haye: Adrian Moetjens, 1682.

_____. *Le Soupé mal apprêté.* Paris: Jules Didot, 1778.

_____. *Crispin médecin.* Paris: Perrault Barbin, 1670.

_____. *Crispin médecin.* Paris: Pierre-Jacques Ribou, 1680.

_____. *Crispin médecin.* La Haye: Adrian Moetjens, 1682.

_____. *Crispin médecin.* Amsterdam: Langerveld, Rotterdam, 1715.

_____. *Crispin médecin.* Amsterdam: Isaac Duim, 1738.

_____. *Crispin médecin.* Paris: N. B. Duchesne, 1774.

_____. *Crispin médecin.* Paris: Pierre-Jacques Ribou, 1767.

_____. *Crispin médecin.* Paris: Pierre-Jacques Ribou, 1770.

Hauteroche. *Crispin médecin*. Paris: Pierre-Jacques Ribou, 1777.

_____. *Crispin médecin*. Paris: Pierre Vente, 1788.

_____. *Crispin médecin*. Paris: Jacques-Charles Brunet, 1789.

_____. *Crispin médecin*. Toulouse: Hacquart C. Devers, 1793.

_____. *Crispin médecin*. Paris: Chez les libraires au théâtre de Molière, 1795.

_____. *Crispin médecin*. Paris: Antoine-Bertrand Fages, 1802.

_____. *Crispin médecin*. Paris: Claude-Bernard M. Petitot, répertoire du théâtre françois, 1804.

_____. *Crispin médecin*. Paris: Claude-Bernard M. Petitot, répertoire du théâtre français, 1818.

_____. *Crispin médecin*. Paris: Comédie-française, 1893.

_____. *Crispin médecin*. Paris: Nicolas Tresse et Pierre-Victor Stock, 1894.

_____. *Crispin médecin*. Paris: Pierre-Victor Stock, 1903.

_____. *Krispyn medicyn*. Amsterdam: Albert Magnus, 1685.

_____. *Krispyn, medicyn*. Amsterdam: P. Rotterdam, 1715.

Hauteroche. *Krispyn, medicyn.* Amsterdam: Isaac Duim, 1738.

_____. *Crispin Lakei og Doktor.* Copenhagen: Skuespil til Brug for den danske Skueplads, 1787.

_____. *Crispin Lakei og Doktor.* Copenhagen: Trykt paa Gyldendals forlag, 1787.

_____. *Crispin médecin.* Copenhagen: Skuespiltekster fra komediehuseti Lille Grønnegade, 1921.

_____. "Crispin médecin." *Les Contemporains de Molière.* Éd. Victor Fournel. Paris: Firmin Didot, 1866.

_____. *Doctor Crispin.* Trans. Edwin L. Isley. Ed. Deborah E. Duncan-Rankin. Charleston, South Carolina: Seventeenth-century Press, 2014.

_____. *Les Apparences trompeuses ou les maris infidèles.* Paris: Pierre Promé, 1673.

_____. *Les Apparences trompeuses.* La Haye: Adrian Moetjens, 1682.

_____. *Les Apparences trompeuses.* Paris: N. B. Duchesne, 1765.

_____. *Le Deuil.* Paris: Pierre Promé, 1673.

_____. *Le Deuil.* Paris: Henry Loyson, 1673.

Hauteroche. *Le Deuil.* Paris: Pierre Promé, 1680.

_____. *Le Deuil.* Paris: Pierre-Jacques Ribou, 1680.

_____. *Le Deuil.* La Haye: Adrian Moetjens, 1682.

_____. *Le Deuil.* Paris: N. B. Duchesne, 1774.

_____. *Le Deuil.* Paris: Claude-Bernard M. Petitot, répertoire du théâtre françois, 1804.

_____. *Le Deuil.* Paris: Répertoire général du théâtre français, 1818.

_____. *Le Deuil.* Paris: Théâtre du XVIIe siècle. Éd. Jacques Truchet. Paris: Gaston Gallimard, 1986.

_____. *Crispin musicien.* Paris: Pierre Promé, 1674.

_____. *Crispin musicien.* Paris: Pierre Promé, 1680.

_____. *Crispin musicien.* Paris: Pierre-Jacques Ribou, 1705.

_____. "Crispin musicien." *Les Contemporains de Molière.* Éd. Victor Fournel. Paris: Firmin Didot, 1866.

_____. *Krispin, muzikant.* Amsterdam: Albert Magnus, 1685.

_____. *Krispyn, muzikant.* Amsterdam: Hendrik Bosch, 1727.

_____. *Krispyn, muzikant.* Amsterdam: Isaac Duim, 1739.

Hauteroche. *Les Nobles de province*. Lyon: Thomas Amaulry, 1678.

_____. *Les Nobles de province*. La Haye: Adrian Moetjens, 1682.

_____. *La Dame invisible*. Paris: Quay des Augustins, 1685. [pirated Pierre-Jacques Ribou printing]

_____. *L'Esprit folet ou la dame invisible*. Paris: Pierre-Jacques Ribou, 1685.

_____. *L'Esprit folet ou la dame invisible*. Paris: Pierre-Jacques Ribou, 1698.

_____. *L'Esprit follet ou la dame invisible*. Paris: Pierre-François Gueffier, 1770.

_____. *L'Esprit follet ou la dame invisible*. Paris: Fin du répertoire du théâtre français, 1824

_____. *L'Esprit follet ou la dame invisible*. Paris: Chez tous les libraires, 1878.

_____. *Le Cocher*. Paris: Quay des Grands Augustins, 1685. [pirated Pierre-Jacques Ribou printing]

_____. *Le Cocher*. Paris: Pierre-Jacques Ribou, 1685.

_____. *Le Cocher*. Paris: Thomas Guillain, 1685.

Hauteroche. *Le Cocher*. Paris: Aux Dépens de la compagnie, 1752.

_____. *Le Cocher supposé*. Avignon: Jean-Louis Chambeau, 1774.

_____. *Le Cocher supposé*. Paris: Antoine-Bertrand Fages, 1802.

_____. *Le Cocher supposé*. Paris: Répertoire général du théâtre français, 1818.

_____. *Le Cocher supposé*. Paris: Madame Veuve Dabo, 1823.

_____. *Le Feint Polonais ou la veuve impertinente*. Lyon: Léonard Plaignard, 1686.

_____. *Les Bourgeoises de qualité*. Paris: Veuve Louis Gontier, 1691.

_____. *Les Bourgeoises de qualité*. Berlin: Robert Roger, 1692.

ON HAUTEROCHE

Adam, Antoine. *Histoire de la littérature française au XVIIe
siècle*. 5 vols. Paris: Domat-Montchrestien, 1948-1956.

Anonymous. "Hauteroche." *The Concise Oxford Dictionary of
French Literature*. Ed. Joyce M. H. Reid. Oxford:
Clarendon Press, 1976.

Anonymous. "Hauteroche." *Dictionnaire des lettres
françaises—le dix-septième siècle*. Éd. Cardinal Georges-
François-Xavier-Marie Grente. Paris: Arthème Fayard,
1951.

Anonymous. "Hauteroche." *Dictionnaire des littératures
françaises et étrangères*. Éd. Jacques Demougin. Paris:
Larousse, 1992.

Anonymous. "Hauteroche." *La Comédie-française (1680-
1980)*. Paris: Bibliothèque Nationale, 1980.

Anonymous. "Hauteroche." *Nouvelle biographie générale depuis
les temps les plus reculés jusqu'à nos jours avec les renseignements
bibliographiques et l'indication des sources à consulter*. Éds. M.
Le Dr. Hoefer et M. De Manne. Paris: Firmin-Didot,
1877.

Anonymous. "Hauteroche." *The Oxford Companion to French
Literature*. Eds. Paul Harvey and Janet E. Heseltine.
Oxford: Clarendon Press, 1959.

Antoine, André. *Le Théâtre*. Paris: Les Éditions de France 1932.

Auger, Louis. "Hauteroche." *Bibliographie universelle ancienne et moderne*. Éd. M. M. Michaud. Paris: Louis Vives, 1880. vol. 18.

Babault, B. "Hauteroche." *Annales dramatiques: ou dictionnaire général des théâtres par une société de gens de lettres*. 9 vols. Paris: de Henée, 1808-1812.

Blanc, André. *F. C. Dancourt (1661-1725): La Comédie française a l'heure du Soleil couchant*. Paris: Éditions Jean-Michel Place, 1984.

_____. *Le Théâtre de Dancourt*. 2 vols. Paris: Librairie Honoré Champion, 1977.

Blémont, H. "Hauteroche." *Dictionnaire de biographie française*. Éds. J. Balteau, M. Barroux, et M. Prévost. Paris: Letouzey et Aîné, 1933. vol. 17.

Bonnassies, Jules. *La Comédie-française: histoire administrative (1658-1757)*. Paris: Didier, 1874.

Brereton, Geoffrey. *French Comic Drama from the Sixteenth to the Eighteenth Century*. London: Algernon Methuen, 1977.

Brooks, William, Éd. *Le Théâtre et l'opéra vus par les gazetiers Robinet et Laurent (1670-1678)*. Universitätsstadt Tübingen: Biblio 17, 1993.

Brüggemann, Werner. *Spanisches Theater und Deutsche Romantik*. Münster Westfalen: Aschendorffsche Verlagsbuchhandlung, 1964. vol. 1.

Calame, Alexandre. "Hauteroche." *Dizionario critico della letteratura francese*. Ed. Franco Simone. Torino: Unione Tipografico-Editrice Torinese, 1972. vol. 1.

Campardon, Émile. *Les Comédiens du roi de la troupe française pendant les derniers siècles*. Paris: Honoré Champion, 1879.

Castil-Blaze, François-Henri-Joseph. *Molière musicien: notes sur les œuvres de cet illustre maître, et sur les drames de Corneille, Racine, Quinault, Regnart, Montluc, Mailly, Hauteroche, Saint-Évremont, DuFresny, Palaprat, Dancourt, Lesage, Destouches. J. J. Rousseau, Beaumarchais, etc.; òu se mêlent des considérations sur l'harmonie de la langue française*. 2 vols. Paris: François-Henri-Joseph Castil-Blaze, 1876.

Chappuzeau, Samuel. *Le Théâtre françois : I. De l'Usage de la comédie. II. Des Auteurs qui   soutiennent le théâtre. III. De la Conduite des comédiens*. 3 vols. Lyon: Michel Mayer, 1674.

Curtis, A. Ross. *Crispin 1er: la vie et l'œuvre de Raymond Poisson comédien-poète du XVIIe siècle*. Toronto: University of Toronto Romance Serie 19, 1972.

Deierkauf-Holsboer, Sophie Wilma. *L'Histoire de la mise en scène dans le théâtre français à Paris*. Paris: A. G. Nizet, 1960.

Deierkauf-Holsboer. *Le Théâtre de Bourgogne.* Paris: A.-G. Nizet, 1970. vol. 2.

_____. *Le Théâtre du Marais.* Paris: A.-G. Nizet, 1958. vol. 2.

Despois, Eugene André. *Le Théâtre français sous Louis XIV.* 3ᵉ Édition. Paris: Librairie Louis Christophe François Hachette, 1886.

Émelina, Jean. *Les Valets et les servantes dans le théâtre comique en France de 1610 à 1700.* Grenoble: Presses Universitaires de Grenoble, 1975.

Forestier, Georges. *Le Théâtre dans le théâtre sur la scène française du XVIIᵉ siècle.* Genève: Librairie Droz maison d'édition genevoise, 1981.

Fournel, Victor. *Les Contemporains de Molière: recueil de comédie rares ou peu connues jouées de 1650 à 1680 avec l'histoire de chaque théâtre, des notes et notices biographiques et critiques.* 2 vols. Paris: Firmin Didot, 1866.

_____. *Le Théâtre au XVIIᵉ siècle: La comédie.* Paris: Lecène, Oudin, et Cie, 1892.

Geoffroy, Julien. "Hauteroche, Crispin médecin." *Cours de littérature dramatique ou recueil par ordre de matières des feuilletons.* 2ᵉ édition. Paris: P. Blanchard, 1825. vol. 2.

Gouvernet, Gérard. *Le Type du valet chez Molière et ses successeurs Regnard, Dufresny, Dancourt et Lesage; caractères et évolution.* New York: Peter Lang, 1985.

Gueullette, Jean-Émile. *Notes et souvenirs sur le théâtre italien au XVIIIᵉ siècle.* Paris: Eugénie Droz, 1938.

Guichemerre, Roger. *La Comédie avant Molière (1640-1660).* Paris: Armand Colin, 1972.

Hawkins, Frederick. *Annals of the French Stage from its Origin to the Death of Racine.* 2 vols. New York: Haskell House Publishers, 1970.

Hélard-Cosnier, Colette. "'La Scène est à Paris'... de Calderón à d'Ouville." *Deux siècles de relations hispano-françaises de Commynes à Madame d'Aulnoy: Actes du colloque international du Centre de recherches et d'études comparatistes ibéro-françaises de la Sorbonne nouvelle.* Éd. Daniel-Henri Pageaux. Paris: Harmattan, 1987.

Isley, Edwin L. *Noël Le Breton de Hauteroche: Seventeenth-century Comic Playwright and Actor.* Ann Arbor, Michigan: University Microfilms International, 1998.

Jal, Auguste. "Hauteroche." *Dictionnaire critique de biographie et d'histoire: errata et supplément pour tous les dictionnaires historiques d'après des documents authentiques inédits.* 2ᵉ Éd. Paris: Henri Plon, 1872.

Jasinski, René. "Hauteroche." *Histoire de la littérature française: nouvelle édition revue et complétée par Robert Bossuet, René Fromilhague, René Pomeau et Jacques Robichez.* Paris: A.-G. Nizet, 1965. vol. 1.

Joannides, Alexandre. *La Comédie-Française de 1680 à 1900, dictionnaire général des pièces et des auteurs.* Paris: Henri Plon, 1901.

_____. *La Comédie-Française de 1680 à 1920: tableau des représentations.* Paris: Henri Plon, 1921.

Jurgens, Madeleine. *Documents du Minutier central des notaires de Paris.* Paris: Archives Nationales, 1982.

Karch, Mariel O'Neill. "État présent des études sur la vie de Noël Le Breton, sieur de Hauteroche (1617-1707), comédien dramaturge, suivi de l'inventaire de ses meubles en 1685." *XVIIe siècle.* 96 (1972), pp. 39-54.

Lachèvre, Frédéric. "Hauteroche." *Dictionnaire des recueils collectifs de poésies publiés de 1597 à 1700.* Paris: Henri Leclerc, vol. 3. 1904.

La Grange, Charles Varlet. *Le Registre de la Grange 1659-1685.* Éds. Bert Edward Young et Grace Philputt Young. Réimprimé. 2 vols. Genève: Librairie Droz, 1947.

La Harpe, Jean-François de. *Cours de littérature ancienne moderne.* Paris: Dupont. 1818. vol. 6.

La Harpe. *Lycée ou cours de littérature ancienne et moderne*. Paris: H. Agasse, 1796.

Lancaster, Henry Carrington. *French Dramatic Literature in the Seventeenth Century*. 9 vols. Baltimore: Johns Hopkins University Press, 1929-1942.

_____, Ed. *Five French Farces*. Baltimore, Maryland: Johns Hopkins University Press. 1937.

_____. *Sunset: A History of Parisian Drama in the Last Years of Louis XIV (1701-1715)*. Baltimore: Johns Hopkins University Press, 1945.

_____. *Actors' Roles at the Comédie-Française According to the Répertoire des comédies françoises qui se peuvent joüer en 1685*. Baltimore: Johns Hopkins University Press, 1951.

_____. *The Comédie française 1680-1701: Plays, Actors, Spectators, Finances*. Baltimore: Johns Hopkins University Press, 1941.

_____. *The Comédie française 1701-1774: Plays, Actors, Spectators, Finances*. Philadelphia: The American Philosophical Society, 1951.

La Porte, Joseph. "Théâtre de Hauteroche." *Observateur littéraire*, 1760.

La Vallière, Louis César de la Baume. *Bibliothèque du théâtre françois depuis son origine; contenant un extrait de tous les ouvrages composes pour ce théâtre; depuis les mystères jusqu'aux pièces de Pierre Corneille; une liste chronologique de celles composées depuis cette dernière époque jusqu'à présent; avec deux tables alphabétiques l'une des auteurs et l'autre des pièces.* Dresde: Michel Groell, 1768.

Lemazurier, Pierre David. *Galerie historique des acteurs du théâtre français, depuis 1600 juqu'à nos jours: ouvrage recueilli des mémoires du temps et de la tradition.* Paris: J. Chaumerot, 1810.

Le Moyne, Nicolas-Toussaine. "Hauteroche." *Les Siècles littéraires de la France.* Réimprimé. Genève: Slatkine, 1971. vol. 3.

Léris, Antoine. "Hauteroche." *Dictionnaire portatif des théâtres, contenant l'origine des différents théâtres de Paris.* C. A. Jambert, 1754.

Lintilhac, Eugène. *Histoire générale du théâtre en France—la comédie du dix-septième siècle.* Paris: Ernest Flammarion, 1904.

Loliée, Frédéric. *La Comédie-française: histoire de la maison de Molière.* Paris: Lucien Laveur, 1907.

Lough, John. *Paris Theatre Audiences in the Seventeenth and Eighteenth Centuries.* London: Oxford University Press, 1957.

Lyonnet, Henry. "Hauteroche." *Dictionnaire des comédiens français: biographie, bibliographie,iconographie.* Genève: Bibliothèque de la revue universelle internationale illustrée, 1911. vol. 2.

Mahelot, Laurent. *Le Mémoire de Mahelot, Laurent et d'autres déorateurs de l'Hôtel de Bourgogne et de la Comédie-française au XVIIe siècle.* Éd. Henry Carrington Lancaster. Paris: Honoré Champion, 1910.

Mantzius, Karl. *A History of Theatrical Art in Ancient and Modern Times.* London: Gerald Duckworth, 1905. vol. 4.

Martin, Henri-Jean. *Livre, pouvoirs et société à Paris au XVIIe siècle (1598-1701).* 2 vols. Genève: Librairie Droz, 1969.

Mazouer, Charles. *Le Personnage du naïf dans le théâtre comique du moyen âge à Marivaux.* Paris: Méridiens Klincksieck, 1979.

Mélèse, Pierre. *Répertoire analytique des documents contemporains d'information et de critique concernant le théâtre à Paris sous Louis XIV—1659-1715.* Paris: Librairie Eugénie Droz, 1934.

Molière, Jean-Baptiste Poquelin de. *Œuvres.* Éds. Eugène Despois, Paul Mesnard, et Arthur Desfeuillons. 9 vols. Paris: Librairie Louis Christophe François Hachette, 1873-1900.

Mongrédien, Georges. "Chronologie des troupes qui ont joué à l'Hôtel de Bourgogne (1598-1680)." *Revue d'histoire du théâtre.* I-II, (1953), pp. 160-74.

_____. "Hauteroche." *Dictionnaire biographique des comédiens français du dix-septième siècle.* Paris: Centre national de la recherche scientifique, 1961.

_____. *Les Grands comédiens du XVIIe siècle.* Paris: Émile Chamontin, 1927.

Mouhy, Charles de Fieux. *Tablettes dramatiques, contenant l'abrège de l'histoire du théâtre françois, l'établissement des théâtres à Paris, un dictionnaire des pièces, et l'abrége de l'histoire des auteurs et des acteurs.* Paris: Sébastien Jorry, 1752.

Moureau, François. *Dufresny, auteur dramatique (1657-1724): ouvrage publié avec le concours du Ministère des Universités et de l'Université de Haute Alsace.* Paris: Éditions Méridiens Klincksieck, 1979.

Parfaict, François et Claude Parfait. *Histoire du théâtre françois.* Paris: Pierre-Gilles le Mercier imprimeur-libraire, 1745. vols. 10-13.

Petit de Julleville, Louis. *Histoire de la langue et de la littérature française des origines à 1900.* Paris: Librairie Armand Colin, 1912. vols. 4 and 5.

Philipot, Emmanuel. *La Vie et l'œuvre littéraire de Noël du Fail: gentilhomme breton.* Paris: Librairie Ancienne Honoré Champion, 1914.

Puibusque, Adolphe. *Histoire comparée des littératures espagnole et française: ouvrage qui a remporté le prix proposé par l'académie française au concours extraordinaire de 1842.* Paris: G.-A. Dentu, 1843. vol. 2.

Quérard, Joseph-Marie. "Hauteroche." *La France littéraire ou dictionnaire bibliographique des savants, historiens et gens de lettres de la France, ainsi que des littérateurs étrangers qui ont écrit en français plus particulièrement pendant les XVIIIᵉ et XIXᵉ siècles.* Paris: Firmin Didot, 1830. vol. 4.

Ricord, Alexandre. *Les Fastes de la comédie française et portraits des plus célèbres acteurs qui se sont illustrés, et ceux qui s'illustrent encore sur notre scène.* Paris: Imprimerie de Hocquet, 1822. vol. 2.

Rohde, Karolus. *Noël le Breton. Sieur de Hauteroche. Theil I., Dissertatio Inauauralis Philogica, QUAM, Consensu et auctoritate, Amplissimi Philosophorum Ordinis in Alma Litterarum Universitate Gryphiswaldensi Ad Summos in Philosophia Honores Rite Capessendos Die XXVII.* Kunike, Gryphiswaldiae: Typis Frid. 1877.

Rothchild, James de, Éd. *Les Continuateurs de Loret: lettres en vers de la Gravette de Mayolas, Robinet, Boursault, Perdou de Subliany, Laurent et autres (1665-1689).* Éds. Baron James de Rothchild et Émile Picot. 3 vols. Paris: Rahir et Cⁱᵉ, 1899.

Royer, Alphonse. *Histoire universelle du théâtre*. Paris: A. Franck, 1870. vol. 3.

Seibt, Robert. *Mrs. Centlivre und ihre Quelle Hauteroche*. Berlin: Weidmannsche Buchhandlung, 1910.

Scherer, Jacques. *La Dramaturgie française en France*. Paris: A.-G. Nizet, 1950.

Stone, George Winchester, Jr. and George M. Kahrl. *David Garrick: A Critical Biography*. Southern Illinois University Press, 1979.

Visé, Jean Donneau de, Éd. *Mercure galant*. Mai, juin, juillet, et août, 1672; Octobre, 1677; Janvier, 1678 et Février 1679, Paris: Éditions Gaston Gallimard, 1684.

Voos, Wilhelm. *Hauteroche (Noël Le Breton) 1617 (?)-1707. Schauspieler und Lustspieldichter, Inaugural: Dissertation zur Erlangung des Doktormürde einer Hohen Philosophischen Fakultät der Universität Köln*. Ohligs: Buchdruckerei Carl Bieth, 1927.

Wildenstein, Daniel. *Inventaires après décès d'artistes et de collectionneurs français du XVIIIᵉ siècle, conservés au Minutier central des notaires de la Seine, aux archives nationales*. Paris: Les Beaux-arts, 1967.

Wright, Charles Henry Conrad. *A History of French Literature*. New York: Haskell House, 1969.

Yarrow, P. J. *A Literary History of France.* 1600-1715. New York: William Barnes and Gilbert Clifford Noble, 1967.

SUGGESTED READINGS

Abraham, Claude. *On the Structure of Molière's Comédies-Ballets*. Paris: Biblio 17, 1984.

Adam, Antoine. *L'Âge classique (1624-1660)*. Paris: B. Arthaud, 1968.

Alvarez-Detrell, Tamara and Michael Paulson. *The Gambling Mania on and off the Stage in Pre-Revolutionary France*. Washington, D.C.: University Press of America, 1982.

Attinger, Gustave. *L'Esprit de la commedia dell'arte dans le théâtre français*. Neuchâtel: La Baconnière, 1950.

Aubrun, Charles Vincent. *La Comedia española (1600-1680)*. Trans. Julio Lago Alonso. Madrid: Taurus, 1968.

Bayard, Françoise. *Le Monde des financiers au XVIIe siècle*. Paris: Ernest Flammarion, 1988.

Bédier, Joseph. *Littérature françaises*. Éd. rév. Paris: Librairie Louis Christophe François Hachette, 1948.

Bénichou, Paul. *Morales du grand siècle*. Paris: Librairie Gaston Gallimard, 1948.

Blue, William R. *The Development of Imagery in Calderón's comédias*. York, South Carolina: Spanish Literature Publications Company, 1983.

Bluche, François. *Louis XIV*. Paris: Arthème Fayard, 1986.

Boursier, Nicole and David Trott, Éds. *L'Âge du théâtre en France*. Edmonton: Academic Publishers, 1988.

Bray, René. *La Préciosité et les précieux*. Paris: Albin Michel, 1945.

Briggs, Robin. *Communities of Belief: Cultural and Social Tensions in Early Modern France*. Oxford: Clarendon Press, 1989.

Caihava d'Estendoux, Jean-Francois. *De l'Ârt de la comédie*. Réimprimé. 2 vols. Genève: Slatkine Reprints, 1970.

Calder, Andrew. *Molière: The Theory and Practice of Comedy*. London: Athlone Press, 1993.

Calderón de la Barca, Pedro. *Primera parte de comedias de Don Pedro Calderón de la Barca*. Ed. Angel Valbuena Briones. Madrid: Clásicos hispánicos, 1974. vol. 1.

Calderón de la Barca, Pedro. *Select Plays of Calderón*. Ed. Norman Maccoll. New York: Palgrave Macmillan, 1888.

Carmody, James Patrick. *Rereading Molière: mise en scène from Antoine to Vitez*. Ann Arbor: University of Michigan Press, 1993.

Chevalley, Silvie. *Album théâtre classique: la vie théâtrale sous Louis XIII et Louis XIV*. Paris: Gallimard-P1éiade, 1970.

Christout, Marie-Françoise. *Le Ballet de cour de Louis XIV, 1643-1672*. Paris: Éditions A. Picard et J. Picard, 1967.

Cohn, Norman. *Europe's Inner Demons*. New York: Basic Books, 1975.

Conesa, Gabriel. *Le Dialogue moliéresque: étude stylistique et dramaturgique*. Paris: Presses universitaires de France, 1983.

Corneille, Pierre. *Théâtre complet*. Éd. Alain Niderst. 3 vols. Rouen: L'Université de Rouen, 1985.

Cowles, William L., Ed. *The Adelphoe of Terence*. Boston: Leach, Shewell, and Sanborn, 1896.

Curtis, A. Ross. "Le Valet Crispin et le premier grand interprète du rôle au XVIIe siècle." *Romanisch Forschungen*. Ed. Vittorio Klostermann Verlag. vol. 78. 1966. pp. 372-382.

D'Amat, Jean-Charles Roman. "Dennebault." *Dictionnaire de biographie française*. Éds. J. Balteau, M. Barroux, et M. Prévost. Paris: Letouzey et Aîné, 1933. vol. 10.

Dancourt, Florent Carton. *La Comédie de Dancourt 1685-1714*. Paris: G. Charpentier, 1882.

_____. *Le Chevalier à la mode*. Éd. Robert H. Crawshaw. Exeter: University of Exeter, 1980.

Dancourt. *Comédies*. Ed. André Blanc. 2 vols. Paris: A.-G. Nizet, 1985.

_____. *Les Bourgeoises de qualité ou la fête de village*. Paris: M. Lecouvreur, 1808.

Defaux, Gérard. *Molière ou les métamorphoses du comique: de la comédie morale au triomphe de la folie*. 2nd Ed. Lexington, Kentucky: French Forum, 1983.

Dessert, Daniel. *Argent, pouvoir et société au grand siècle*. Paris: Arthème Fayard, 1984.

Devlin, Judith. *The Superstitious Mind: French Peasants and the Supernatural in the Nineteenth Century*. New Haven: Yale University Press, 1987.

Duchêne, Roger. "La Veuve au XVIIe siècle." *Onze études sur l'image de la femme dans la littérature française du dix-septième siècle*. Éd. Wolfgang Leiner. Paris: Jean-Michel Place, 1928. pp. 221-42.

DuFail, Noël. *Contes et discours d'Eutrapel*. 2 vols. Réimprimé. D. Jouaust. Paris: Librairie des bibliophiles, 1875.

Elam, Keir. *The Semiotics of Theatre and Drama*. London: Algernon Methuen, 1980.

Fairclough, Henry Rushton, Trans. *Horace: Satires, Epistles and Ars Poetica*. Cambridge: Harvard University Press, 1966.

Forestier, Georges. *Molière*. Paris: Bordas, 1990.

Froldi, Rinaldo. *Il Teatro valenzano e l'origine della commedia barocca*. Pisa: Editrice Tecnico Scientifica, 1962.

Furetière, Antoine. *Le Roman bourgeois: romanciers du XVIIe siècle*. Paris: Gallimard-Pléiade, 1958.

Gaines, James F. *Social Structures in Molière's Theatre*. Columbus, Ohio: The Ohio State University Press, 1984.

Garapon, Robert. *La Fantaisie verbale et le comique dans le théâtre français du moyen âge à la fin du XVIIe siècle*. Paris. 1957.

Garrick, David. *The Lying Valet*. Microprint. London: John Dicks, 1864-1872. vol. 6.

Gros, Étienne. *Philippe Quinault: sa vie et son œuvre*. Paris: Honoré Champion. 1926.

Hall, H. Gaston. *Le Bourgeois gentilhomme: Context and Stagecraft*. Durham: University of Durham, 1990.

_____. *Comedy in Context: Essays on Molière*. Jackson, Mississippi: University Press of Mississippi, 1984.

Herzel, Roger W. "The Décor of Molière's Stage: The Testimony of Brissart and Chauveau." *Proceedings of the Modern Language Association*. 93, (1978), pp. 925-54.

Hollier, Denis, et al., Eds. *A New History of French Literature.* Cambridge: Harvard University Press, 1989.

Howarth, William Driver, Ed. *Comic Drama: The European Heritage.* London: Algernon Methuen, 1978.

_____. *Molière: A Playwright and His Audience.* Cambridge: Cambridge University Press, 1982.

_____, Ed. *Molière: Stage and Study; Essays in Honour of W. G. Moore.* Oxford: Clarendon Press, 1973.

Jasinski, René. *Histoire de la littérature française.* 2 vols. Paris: Boivin, 1947.

Jouvet, Louis. *Molière et la comédie classique.* Paris: Gaston Gallimard, 1965.

Kennard, Joseph S. *Masks and Marionettes.* New York: Palgrave Macmillan Company, 1935.

Knutson, Harold. *Molière: An Archetypal Approach.* Toronto: University of Toronto Press, 1976.

_____. *The Triumph of Wit: Molière and Restoration Comedy.* Columbus, Ohio: The Ohio State University Press, 1988.

Lanson, Gustave. "Molière et la farce." *Revue de Paris.* 1901. vol. 3, pp. 129-53.

La Rochefoucauld, François de. *Maximes*. Éd. Jacques Truchets. Paris: Garnier, 1967.

Lawrenson, Thomas Edward. *The French Stage in the 17th Century: A Study of the Advent of the Italian Order*. Manchester: Manchester University Press, 1954.

Leman, Michel. *Les Valets et les servantes dans le théâtre comique en France de 1610 à 1700*. Ed. Jean Émelina. Cannes: Presses Universitaires de France, 1975.

Lemoine, Jean. La *Des Œillets: une grande comédienne, une maitresse de Louis XIV*. Paris: Perrin, n.d. [1938]

Lough, John. *Seventeenth-Century French Drama: The Background*. Oxford: Clarendon, 1979.

Marion, Marcel. *Dictionnaire des institutions de la France aux XVIIe et XVIIIe siècles*. Paris: Picard, 1979.

Martineche, Ernest. *La Comédia espagnole en France de Hardy à Racine*. Paris: Louis Christophe François Hachette, 1900.

Mélèse, Pierre. *Le Théâtre et son public à Paris sous Louis XIV*. Genève: Librairie Droz, 1934.

Molière, Jean-Baptiste Poquelin de. *Œuvres complètes de Molière*. Ed. René Bray. 3 vols. Paris: Club du meilleur livre, 1954.

Molière, Jean-Baptiste Poquelin de. *Œuvres complètes*. Ed. Robert Jouanny. 2 vols. Paris: Garnier, 1962.

_____. *Les Femmes savantes*. Ed. H. Gaston Hall. Oxford: Clarendon Press, 1974.

Mongrédien, Georges. *Daily Life in the French Theatre at the Time of Molière*. Trans. Claire E. Engel. London: George Allen and Unwin, 1969.

_____. *La Vie privée de Molière*. Paris: Librairie Louis Christophe François Hachette, 1950.

_____. *La Vie quotidienne des comédiens au temps de Molière*. Paris: Louis Christophe François Hachette, 1966.

Montfleury, Antoine Jacob. *La Femme juge et partie*. Paris: Delalain, 1774.

_____. *Le Mary sans femme*. Ed. Edward Forman. Exeter: University of Exeter, 1985.

Moore, W. G. "Molière's Theory of Comedy." *L'Esprit créateur*. vol. 6 (1966), pp. 137-45.

Moraud, Yves. *Masques et jeux dans le théâtre comique en France entre 1685 et 1730*. Paris: Honoré Champion, 1977.

Mornet, Daniel. *Histoire de la littérature française classique, 1660-1700: ses caractères véritables, ses aspects inconnus*. 3e Éd. Paris: Colin, 1947.

Mousnier, Roland E. *The Institutions of France under the Absolute Monarchy, 1598-1789*. Trans. Brian Pearce. 2 vols. Chicago: University of Chicago Press, 1979.

Niemeyer, Charles. "The Hôtel de Bourgogne, France's First Popular Playhouse." *The Theatre Annual* (1947): 64-80.

Osborne, Nancy F. *The Doctor in the French Literature of the Sixteenth Century*. Mornings Heights: King's Crown Press, 1946.

Ouville, Antoine le Métel d'. *L'Élite des contes du sieur d'Ouville*. 2 vols. Réimprimé. L'Édition de Rouen 1680. Paris: Librairie des bibliophiles, 1883.

_____. *L'Esprit folet*. Paris: Toussaint Quinet, 1642.

Pascal, Blaise. *Pensées*. Éd. Louis Lafuma. Paris: Édition du seuil, 1962.

Phillips, Henry. *The Theatre and its Critics in Seventeenth-century France*. Oxford: Clarendon, 1980.

Piatt, Charles. *Popular Superstitions*. Rpt. Detroit: Gale Research Company, 1973.

Poisson, Raymond. *Les Œuvres complètes de Raymond Poisson*. Paris: Pierre-Jacques Ribou, 1678.

_____. *Le Baron de la Crasse et l'après-soupé des auberges*. Éd. Charles Mazouer. Paris: A.-G. Nizet, 1987.

Pomeau, René. *L'Âge classique*. 1680-1715. Paris: B. Arthaud, 1971.

Quinault, Philippe. *Théâtre choisi*. Paris: Laplace, Sanchez, et Cie, 1882.

Radford, E. and M. A. Radford. *Encyclopaedia of Superstitions*. New York: The Philosophical Library, 1949.

Racine, Jean. *Œuvres complètes*. Éd. Pierre Clarac. Paris: Le Seuil-l'intégrale, 1962.

Réaux, Gédéon Tallemant des. *Historiettes*. Ed. Antoine Adam. 2 vols. Paris: Gallimard-Pléiade, 1958.

Rousset, Jean. *La Littérature de l'âge baroque en France: Circé et le paon*. Paris: Corti, 1954.

Saulnier, F. "Les Comédiens à Rennes au XVIIe siècle, documents inédits." *Bulletin et mémoires de la société archéologique du Département d'Ille-et-Vilaine*. 1880.

Scarron, Paul. *Œuvres de Scarron*. 7 vols. Paris: Jean François Bastien, 1786.

Scott, Virginia. *The Commedia dell'arte in Paris, 1644-1697*. Charlottesville: University Press of Virginia, 1990.

Sevais, Paul, Éd. *Inventaires après-décès et ventes de meubles: apports à une histoire de la vie économique et quotidienne XIVe-XIXe siècle*. Louvain-la-Neuve: Academia, 1988.

Sévigné Marie de Rabutin-Chantal. *Lettres*. Éd. Roger
Duchêne. 3 vols. Paris: Gallimard-Pléiade, 1978.

Simon, Alfred, Éd. *Molière par lui-même*. Paris: Éditions du
seuil, 1967.

_____. *Molière: une vie*. Lyon: La Manufacture, 1988.

Tobin, Ronald W. "Le Misanthrope revu et corrigé : Le
Philinte de Fabre d'Églantine." Gabriel Marcoux-
Chabot, Pézenas, France, 2009.

_____. *Tarte à la Crème: Comedy and Gastronomy in Moliere's
Theater*. Columbus: The Ohio State University Press,
1990.

Vanuxem, Jacques. "Le Décor de théâtre sous Louis XIV."
Dix-septième siècle. 39 (1958), pp. 196-216.

Visé, Jean Donneau de. *Trois comédies*. Paris: Librairie
Eugénie Droz, 1940.

Walker, Hallam. *Molière*. Boston: Twayne Publishers, 1990.

Williams, Charles G. S. "Doubling and Omission in the
Text of Anne Ferrand's *Bélise*." *Convergences: Rhetoric and
Poetic in Seventeenth-Century France: Essays for Hugh M.
Davidson*. Eds. David Lee Rubin and Mary B. McKinley.
Columbus, Ohio: The Ohio State University Press,
1989. pp. 123-43.

Williams, Charles G. S. *Madame de Sévigné*. Boston: Twayne
    Publishers, 1981.

Zuber, Roger et Micheline Cuénin. *Le Classicisme (1660-
    1680)*. Paris: B. Arthaud, 1984.

The Coachman

Noël Le Breton de Hauteroche

The Coachman

Noël Le Breton de Hauteroche